CHRISTIE'S

world of

automotive

TOYS

MIKE AND SUE RICHARDSON

MBI Publishing Company

This edition first published in 1998 by **MBI Publishing Company,**

729 Prospect Avenue, PO Box 1, Osceola, WI 54020-0001 USA.

text © mike and sue richardson

PHOTOGRAPHS KINDLY SUPPLIED BY: **mike and sue richardson**

and christie's south kensington

SPECIAL PHOTOGRAPHY: **ed schneider**

DESIGN: **balley design associates**

DESIGNERS: **simon balley and joanna hill**

First published in Great Britain in 1998 by **Pavilion Books, Ltd.**

The information in this book is true and complete to the best of our knowledge. All recommendations are made without any guarantee on the part of the author or publisher, who also disclaim any liability incurred in connection with the use of this data or specific details.

We recognize that some words, model names, and designations, for example, mentioned herein are the property of the trademark holder. We use them for identification purposes only. This is not an official publication.

MBI Publishing Company books are also available at discounts in bulk quantity for industrial and sales-promotional use. For details write to Special Sales Manager at Motorbooks International Wholesalers & Distributors, 729 Prospect Avenue, PO Box 1, Osceola, WI 54020-0001 USA.

Library of Congress Cataloging-in-Publication Data Available.

ISBN 0-7603-0569-2

Printed in Italy by Conti Tipocolor.

c o n t e n t s

From the moment the first internal combustion engine was fitted to a wheeled vehicle in the 1880s to create the 'horseless carriage', it was only a matter of time before the toy makers followed suit. Sure enough, when Henry Ford made the first automobiles around the turn of the century and children started enjoying the sight of these noisy contraptions that began to appear everywhere, there was an immediate demand for toys cars.

INTROD

It was a relatively straightforward matter for the toy manufacturers to add to their existing catalogues. After all, if you could make a cast-iron horse-drawn item with turning wheels, you could make a cast-iron automobile with turning wheels; if you could make a pressed-steel hansom cab, you could make a pressed-steel doctor's coupé – and American toy manufacturers, led by the Dayton Group in Ohio, did just that. German and French industries, already skilled in producing fine mechanical toys, also had no difficulty adapting to the new demand. Cheaper toys were not neglected either, and Pennytoys (five- and ten-cent toys) from France and Germany quickly penetrated the markets on either side of the Atlantic.

In the early days (1890–1920), whether made of wood, cast iron or tin, the toys were not recognizable as any particular make. By the time of World War I, some were powered. A flywheel system developed in the US produced effective forward momentum at the slightest push; in Germany clockwork vehicles were made by

UCTION

Lehmann, Bing, Günthermann and Hess, and steam-driven ones were made by Carette. After the war, American toy manufacture really came into its own, and the actual vehicles seen on the roads were reproduced with ever-greater fidelity, mostly using pressed steel and cast iron, by Buddy L, Arcade and Marx.

The range of toys had been wide from the start; children had always taken great pleasure in 'commercials' – trucks, vans and buses with decals of names and adverts applied on to the sides – and fire engines, diggers, earth movers and farm vehicles. These were joined by cars of all kinds, from Rolls and Cadillacs to sports and racing cars. Most popular of all were working models with moving parts, action features or gimmicks, such as the Elgin road-sweeper that actually swept and the motorcycle whose rider leapt in and out of the saddle – vehicles that anticipated the sophisticated radio-controlled models of today.

The process of pressure diecasting in mazac, and later plastic, was used in the US in the1930s by Tootsietoy and Hubley, and after World War II by Ertl and Marx, using aluminium and plastic respectively. In England the new process was adopted by Dinky; in Germany by Marklin. Now it was possible to mass-produce high-quality toys cheaply and still achieve great accuracy of modelling, especially when the toys were sold under licence from the manufacturers of the full-size versions. Thereafter, what had always been sold as toys for children began, significantly, to appeal to adults as well.

Ironically, it was a time of relative prosperity that brought the greatest pressures to bear on the toy manufacturers. The emergence of the 'teen culture' in the 1960s saw childhood effectively shortened as children, lured away by pop music, fashion and television, grew out of toy cars at an earlier age. Since then, the toy car market has been further squeezed by the end of the population bulge of the baby-boomer generation and by competition from rival attractions such as Action Man and, later, computer games.

The manufacturers have responded in a variety of ways: by amalgamating; by shifting production to the Far East to reduce costs; by specializing in sturdy toys for younger children; and, crucially, by moving away from the toy market and concentrating on producing models for collectors. It had become clear that there was a healthy adult market for miniature gems designed to be displayed rather than played with.

To the collector, however, by far the greatest interest – and value – lies in period items from the toy-making heyday. Remarkably high prices are now paid for good examples, especially scarcer items, at the numerous toy fairs and auctions. However, the higher the prices paid for antique toys and models, the greater

the risk of making an expensive mistake. Owing to the frequency with which older models are reissued, often

even using original moulds and dies, it is not always easy to verify a toy's authenticity. Even in the world of

toy cars, chicanery exists, and collectors need to be on their guard against later versions or reproductions

passed off as originals. As in all antique collecting, the best defence against deception is knowledge.

It is hoped that by outlining the history of toy-car making and by identifying some of the pitfalls awaiting

the unwary, *Christie's World of Automotive*

Toys will be of practical

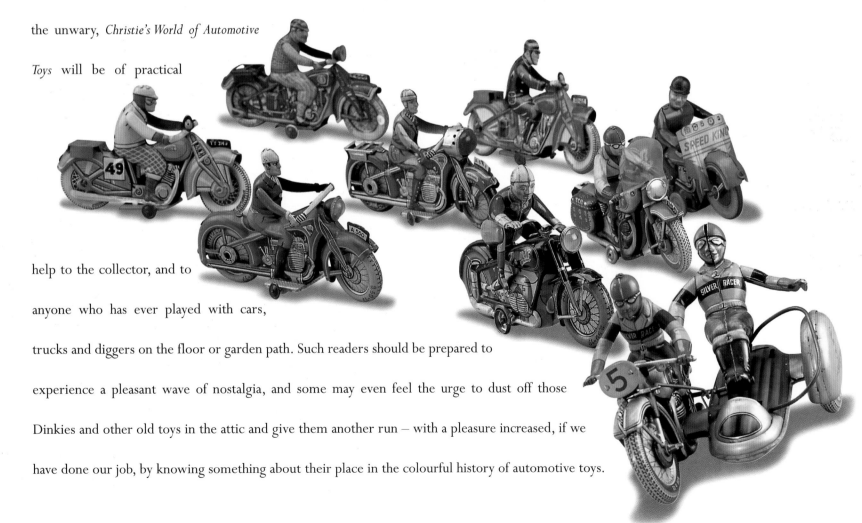

help to the collector, and to

anyone who has ever played with cars,

trucks and diggers on the floor or garden path. Such readers should be prepared to

experience a pleasant wave of nostalgia, and some may even feel the urge to dust off those

Dinkies and other old toys in the attic and give them another run – with a pleasure increased, if we

have done our job, by knowing something about their place in the colourful history of automotive toys.

In the mid-nineteenth century, before Karl Friedrich Benz invented the automobile, the toy industries in Europe and America were busy developing new manufacturing techniques and products. There were marked differences, however, between the two parts of the industrialized world, America and Europe. The United States was a vast, expanding country with an industrial belt across the north between the eastern seaboard and the Great Lakes, with parallel manufacturing regions in Canada. There were ports and cities along the Atlantic coast to the south, and a huge interior of agricultural land, mountains and deserts with isolated industrial and farming settlements. Europe was a jumble of states, each of which was developing its own industry and devoting its time – when the armies were not fighting among themselves or with the rest of the world – to competing economically by aggressively developing and exporting new products.

The sheer size of America, its vast spaces and relatively small population meant that land was fairly cheap compared with Europe, and each farm or house in a rural town was larger than those of the crowded Old World. Machinery and vehicles had to be robust and large to work the American land and to stand up to the rough roads, and the materials from which things were made had to withstand much hard use for many years. American industry was thus used to making artefacts that did not break, or were easily repaired if they did: products farmers could mend themselves or have repaired by the local blacksmith, and which did not have to be sent hundreds of miles to the manufacturers for fixing.

Children's toys are frequently scaled-down versions of the things they are familiar with in the adult world, and even playthings need to be strong to withstand the roughness of the backyard, where children with access to the outside prefer to play. In the US, the existing technologies of manufacturing in wood, pressed steel and cast iron were perfectly fitted for producing suitable toys.

German industry meanwhile, particularly the firm of Lehmann, was perfecting attractive, cheap, light, mass-market tin toys, which they sold as far and wide as they could. The differences between these two production styles meant that European toys supplemented American-made ones, rather than competing with them directly.

For the first twenty-five years after the invention of the automobile, from 1890 to 1914, most of the transatlantic trade travelled from Europe to America, as the growing population of the US became more prosperous and imports augmented the products of the home industry. Around the turn of the century, the demand for toys of all sorts was so great that the value of imports from Germany alone roughly equalled the value of toys produced in the United States. As industry powered prosperity, there was a continual increase in the amount of money available. Henry Ford's Model T – both the actual automobile and the toy versions – became a symbol of that prosperity, and firms in the US as well as overseas developed rapidly to help people spend their new wealth.

WOODEN TOYS

Toys made of wood have existed for centuries. They were easy to make as the raw material was around everywhere. A sharp knife could carve a little animal out of a stick. But because wood breaks easily and burns well, few examples of early wooden toys have survived into the late twentieth century. Luckily, the long distances between town centres in the US had led to the development of mail-order firms and their well illustrated catalogues , so at least we know what was available.

In 1878, one of these new mail-order firms, Montgomery Ward & Co., was advertising wheeled toys. Taylor of Chicago was making a boys' wagon, a small version of a horse-drawn wagon that could carry a load, and there was a whole range of US mail wagons, some of which were big enough to carry a child. These had to be pulled along by other children, but can be regarded as precursors of the pedal car. By 1894, it was advertising a Rescue Hook and Ladder Truck Co. No. 1 that was 'made wholly of wood. Has four handsomely painted ladders, which are so made that they can be joined together, forming one long ladder. An interesting toy for any boy'. This was a pull-along toy, but before long there were models of fire vehicles powered by internal combustion engines. Of the manufacturers themselves, even where they are named in the catalogues, virtually nothing else is known. The main exception is Schoenhut, which is famed for its circus animals. In the years before World War I. Schoenhut featured a range of Modlwood toys tbat had four or five different automotive shapes: open and closed cars, racers and a couple of trucks that 'can be readily put together and taken apart…[giving] plenty of study and constructive amusement'. Wooden vehicles from these early years rarely show up on the collectors' circuit, but examples in good condition with interesting paper stickers are worth collecting.

In Europe, wooden toy production flourished in Germany, especially in the Erzgebirge area of Saxony. After the collapse of the local mining industries, the villagers had taken to the cottage production of wooden items during the winter, and by the 1850s had organized themselves into guilds. They exhibited at the Nuremberg Toy Fair, and their products, especially Noah's Arks and animals, came to be known by the name Erzgebirge. With the advent of the automobile, it was simple to add toy road vehicles to their range.

below: *The first Tootsietoy car, no. 4528, (5cm/2in, 1911, USA) surrounded by European flat-lead vehicles.*

CAST-IRON TOYS

At the end of the nineteenth century American toys were characteristically manufactured in cast iron. Not only was it used for a great variety of playthings, but its use was almost exclusive to America. Toy automobile collectors have hunted widely for European firms that specialized in cast iron and have come up with an insignificant handful. The technology of casting in iron was perfect for a country that had not yet completed its Industrial Revolution, a country that had to concentrate on developing the land and feeding the towns, rather than on making sophisticated machinery that could weave fine cloth, make small intricate parts for watches for the luxury market, and produce repeat quantities of goods for export.

centre: *A clockwork-motored Bing Open Tourer, missing its driver (tinplate, 27cm/10.5in, c1914, Germany).*

While the technology for cast iron was known to the ancient Chinese, it was developed to a high degree of sophistication during the Industrial Revolution in England – the materials needed to make cast iron are iron ore, fuel for smelting and water for cooling. There are iron ore deposits around the Great Lakes, especially on the upper side of Lake Superior. The heartland of manufacturing was further south in Detroit and Cleveland on Lake Erie and in Chicago on Lake Michigan – all areas with water transport for the raw materials. Not only was cast iron easy to make, it was readily transportable to the factories, which made items of all sizes: locomotive wheels, girders and framing for skyscrapers, farm implements, cylinders for steam engines, stands for sewing machines, wheels for prams, domestic fire grates, decorative stands for kettles... and toys.

The iron-casting process is also relatively simple. A tray of sand incorporating a gluing medium takes the impression of a full-size wooden model of the desired piece (say, a house name plate) as easily as wax takes that of a seal ring. Cast iron is added by gravity, allowed to cool and broken out of the sand. Multi-piece moulds allow more complex pieces to be made in a similar way. Gravity filling of moulds has its limitations, because air bubbles tend to collect in corners and undercuts are difficult, so large or complicated cast-iron items are often made in pieces and then fastened together. This generally results in products that are heavy and robust. The low technology of the foundry was ideal for short-run productions of large, low-demand items like locomotive wheels, but if it were necessary to make enough sewing-machines stands to equip a garment factory, one could increase production just by adding another shed and employing more labour. It is also possible to make cast-iron articles with more intricate detail, but they are correspondingly more expensive, as better-quality iron, made with low-impurity coke, is needed, and more care has to be taken in the making and filling of the moulds.

The 1886 Montgomery Ward catalogue advertised a wide variety of toys made from cast iron. At the simple, cheap end is a twenty-four-piece set of solid menagerie animals, including elephants, giraffes and chickens, 2.5 to 7cm (1–3in) long. Toys on wheels manufactured by the Gong Bell company range from a simple pull-along bell sounded by a cam on the axle, to an elaborate Liberty Chime, which portrayed Liberty riding like Venus on a shell, waving the Stars and Stripes! A less fanciful method of transport is represented by an iron money-box in the form of a San Francisco-type cable car, which was set in motion when a coin was dropped in the top. The catalogue also has a selection of 'indestructible malleable iron toys' – a horse-drawn truck with driver and load 32cm (13in) long and an even larger fire engine at 45cm (18in). The cast-iron toy manufacturers were not going to have the slightest difficulty adapting production to models of vehicles powered by the newly introduced internal combustion engine.

STEEL AND TINPLATE TOYS

In the US, when steel was incorporated into toys, it was frequently used along with cast iron and made up only a small part of the toy, notably the bell for chime toys and perhaps a carriage seat or the body of a cart. Usually quite heavy-gauge, the steel was therefore difficult to make into complicated shapes; it is not really surprising that cast iron was so much more popular.

The European version of sheet steel used for toys was tinplate. This is a very thin sheet of steel coated with tin; its attractive shiny finish provided a good surface, if first etched, for paint or for colourful litho printing. Offset lithography had developed into a reliable and repeatable process by which a pattern was transferred from the original lithographic stone, via a flat plate or, later, rubber rollers, to the surface of the tin. This could then be cut and folded into a variety of shapes, from a simple biscuit tin to the cleverest mechanical Lehmann toy. Most of the steel toys sold in the US were these light tinplate ones imported from Germany. It was easier, at this time, to ship consignments across the Atlantic than across the US. The vast interiors were reached mainly by railroad. Whereas in Europe complex road networks were already in place before the automobile arrived, in America their development followed that of automotive transport.

below: *A pressed-steel and cast-iron Hill Climber Two-seater Car with friction motor (30cm/12in, c1903, USA).*

MAKERS AND SELLERS

Once the processes for making the toys had developed and merchandise was available, it had to be sold. In the US, unlike in Europe, specialist shops were few and far between, a notable example being the famous F.A.O. Schwartz of New York City, established in 1862 and still active today. Smaller toy outlets such as hardware stores were supplied by wholesale companies, among them Butler Bros and Marshall Field & Co, which had cohorts of travelling salesmen and sent out trade catalogues. But daily or even weekly town shopping was out of the question for many Americans, and they relied on mail-order companies such as Montgomery Ward & Co., which started in 1872, and Sears Roebuck, which began in the early 1890s. The illustrated catalogues of these middle men provided much of our knowledge about early American toys. We know the size, the weight, the mechanical action, the packing quantity, and the price – but often not the name of the manufacturer. The distribution companies that were doing the advertising and selling were much more powerful than the makers, who would go to them cap-in-hand to demonstrate the superior qualities of their products.

Occasionally, a catalogue states that the toys were 'imported from Germany', or were 'quality European toys', but rarely was the source specified. Until toy collectors had the chance to commit time to research, we knew what was for sale but not who made it. This lack of information is not helped by the absence of identifying marks on many toys, whatever material they were made from. The name would have meant nothing to the original purchaser, and applying it might have damaged the look of the toy or just made the item cost more. Even the decorative as well as informative trademarks, which were so common on European toys, were not much used in America. Some collectors say that it should not matter who made a toy, that its desirability lies in its attractiveness, its working features or its play value. Most people, however, are curious and want to know as much as possible, including the maker's name. Manufacturers who made desirable toys gained recognition, and today being able to name the maker nowadays usually enhances a toy's value.

THE DAYTON GROUP

The Dayton Group, as it was referred to, was a loose association of Ohio toy companies. Patient research by several collectors has revealed that D. P. Clark first set up business in 1897. In 1904, he was joined by Schieble, but four years later, Schieble left to set up the Schieble Toy and Novelty Co. with John C. Turner, who later departed from Schieble to set up business on his own. Clark meanwhile renamed his firm the Dayton Friction Toy Works. While this history led to the companies being labelled the Dayton Group, the interactions and disagreements between the individuals and their companies resulted in many differences in their products.

The toys that the Dayton Friction Toy Works produced are known as Hill Climber Friction Power Toys, a type that remained in production until the Great Depression took its toll on the nation's toy industry. The Toy Works' significant era was before World War I, because it was the first manufacturer to develop a particularly American mechanism with which to fight off the inroads of European clockwork toys.

In 1897, Clark patented a rotating flywheel system that gave the toys great momentum across uncarpeted wooden floors. As the 1903 Montgomery Ward catalogue tells us:

All Hill Climber toys are now equipped with a new patent 'Self Adjustable Friction Distributing Idler' which presses together the working parts and causes the power axle to bite and grip at every touch. The slightest touch starts the toy, and by pressing down and giving two or three hard pushes, sufficient momentum will be given to the power to travel a long distance. It runs backward and forward, up hill or down hill and over small obstructions with ease. It may be used outdoors as well as in and furnishes unlimited amusement to children of all ages.

Clark's early toys – for instance an automobile in the style of 'the latest and most fashionable', complete with a chauffeur and two lady passengers in big hats; a fire engine with moving piston rod, pump wheel and gong 'giving an air of hustle and bustle to the toy so necessary to imitate a real fire engine'; a circus menagerie wagon that 'contains five animals each of which moves cleverly around in the cage as it runs on the floor' – were made of hand-soldered tin painted in bright colours with gilt striping. The chassis, flywheel and large wheels, positioned so close together that they were almost touching, were made of cast iron.

Other Dayton Group manufacturers made clockwork-powered trucks with a more conventional wheelbase – one at each corner – and some had rubber-tyred wheels. All of these were generic toys, however, not particular models. As the years passed, more realistic models joined the ranges, and 'early' and 'late' items are featured in the same catalogue. A 1915 advert had the above-mentioned fire engine and menagerie wagon, but also current phaetons and tourers, along with panel vans,

trucks and tanks that look as strange as the originals. The toys have increased in length from 20 to 5cm (8–10in) up towards 40 to 50cm (16–20in) and have details pressed into the tin rather than being painted on. Many have separate wings-cum-running-boards attached to the sides.

RIVALS

The Dayton Group did not have a clear field for long. Acme, whose trademark was a stencilled A monogram, made an excellent representation of a 1900 Curved Dash Oldsmobile.

This is perhaps the earliest *model* car made in America. Other pressed-steel toy manufacturers stayed in business for longer. Ives made toys of the old-fashioned horseless carriage sort from 1907, before concentrating on trains. Hafner similarly was the ancestor of American Flyer trains. The Wilkins Toy Company, which manufactured in steel and cast iron, was acquired by the famous firm of Kingsbury.

There was also the challenge of toys imported from Europe, particularly from Germany. Lehmann products are often named as such in the American catalogues, and other manufacturers are clearly recognizable from the good illustrations of the toys. Bassett-Lowke steam cars are oddly priced in sterling in 1903/4, as are the more expensive clockwork versions of the toys. A wide variety of Bing vehicles was also imported. Hess, with its distinctive smaller models, is easy to recognize. Top-of-the-range Carette limousines, with a chauffeur and trunks on the roof, are in the catalogues too. Indeed, in 1914 about half of all toys sold in America were of German origin.

Increasingly, American toys were advertised as American: 'guaranteed domestic mechanical toys', which were being powered by clockwork, just like German toys. One manufacturer claimed that they 'Run on entirely new principles, guaranteed spiral springs on steel shaft adjusted to series of cogs, run 150ft with 1 winding. Fine enamel and each with chauffeur, front wheels turn', so that the toys could run in circles. There was also a Flying Racer and a Flying Limousine, both finished in lavender and red with gilt stripes. While it sounds as if these were painted tin, at least one manufacturer was making automotive toys from lithographed tin.

centre: *A fully restored American National Automobiles No. 7 Child's Pedal Car (107cm/42in, c1910, USA).*

above: *The Bing Brake with clockwork motor and leather seat cushions (tinplate, 25cm/10", c1902, Germany).*

At the turn of the century, Ferdinand Strauss, regarded by many writers to be the founder of the mechanical toy industry in America, was an importer of German toys. As the realization grew that the US was losing out to Europe, Strauss began to make clockwork, litho tin toys of light weight and good quality to compete head to head and to supply his own toy shops. By 1914, he was producing beautifully made toys to fill the shelves of his four New York shops. The toys were fragile and few have survived, making them much sought-after by collectors.

American catalogues also offered pedal cars made of pressed steel. A 1914 Butler Bros catalogue features 'Juvenile Steel Automobiles: All up-to-date ′models, handsomely finished, sheet steel bodies, auto steering system, open bottoms, strong double spoke wheels'. These range in size from 75cm (30in) to 125cm (50in) long and sport names such as

Scorcher, National, Wizard and Speedwell. If you found the remains of one in a junk shop, you would have no trouble dating it to before World War I, for they catch the high-perched, open-box look of the runabouts of the time. Surprisingly, none of this group looks very like a model of the full size. The Ford Model T was selling so well that many children would have given anything for a pedal version.

CAST IRON PREDOMINATES

Today, the most visible production from this era is in cast iron, partly because a lot of it was made and partly because of its indestructibility. This feature, which has always been valued highly by parents, was heavily promoted in advertising, and it is true that a cast-iron toy would survive rough treatment in an unpaved back yard. You can often tell the 'play value' of a toy (how much it has been played with) by how much of the original paint is left, and it is not unusual to find that it has disappeared from almost all of the outer surfaces. To determine the factory colour you will need to inspect the inside of the toy in a good light or with a pencil torch. If the model, say an excavator, has spent much time buried in a sand tray, however, whatever paint is left may be badly faded.

The material is not just heavy but brittle, and thin wings and other small unsupported pieces can break off if the toy is dropped on a pavement or hard surface. It is fairly common now to find that a damaged chassis has been replaced by a new one, perhaps made from lead or even from cast iron. One giveaway is that the toy is now held together with screws instead of the original rivets. But there are some skilled restorers around, who can do an excellent job of replacing parts so that they look original. Though the work can take a long time, the reward is the enormous difference in price between a broken toy and one that looks factory-fresh. Unfortunately, a meaningless phrase has crept into sales lists: 'restored to original'. A toy can be original, or restored, but not both. A restored or repainted toy is never worth as much as an original.

For the first twenty or so years of toy vehicle production, cast-iron toys tended to be big, but during the next twenty years, as many as four, six or even more sizes of the same type were made. The toys reflected the transport of the time, and as body styles changed in the full-size world, the models changed as well. Once an item appeared in a catalogue, however, it was often kept there long after the style had been superseded. This makes dating difficult. It is often possible to say that an item with a particular cab shape cannot be earlier than X, but unless there is manufacturer's catalogue evidence, it is not possible to attribute a not-later-than-X date. The earliest makers of cast-iron toy-autos, Dent and Williams, did not mark their products either, though Kenton sometimes did. During this period, the toys were occasionally fitted with clockwork motors and could wreak terrible

damage on furniture if they got out of control. These motors were often 'bought out', as were wheels, and may be little help in identifying the manufacturer of a toy.

AMERICAN MANUFACTURERS

A. C. Williams, a long-established family firm in Ravena, Ohio, turned to toy making in 1893. Kenton of Kenton, Ohio, and the Dent Hardware Co. of Fullerton, Pennsylvania, were established in 1894 and 1895 respectively. Who made the first automotive toy is a matter for speculation.

below: *A Märklin Motor Fire Engine with clockwork motor and steering (tinplate, 28cm / 11in, c1910, Germany).*

Williams is well known for its range of horse-drawn fire appliances modelled with horses racing to put out the flames. It made money-boxes and smaller cast-iron pieces as well as some automotive items. Their trucks, sedans and tourers are unmarked, but feature turned-steel wheel hubs. These are prevented from slipping off the axles by the spreading effect of the iron axle rod being hit on the end with a starred peen. The firm survived the 1930s depression by making dime-store toys.

Dent and his partners expanded their hardware business into toys around the turn of the century, producing very fine castings. Their vehicles are crisply detailed and fitted with wheels much smaller than those of their competitors. Even as early as 1909, two Dent products – a car and a fire pumper – featured wings and running boards, and the vehicles, at about 35cm (14in) long, are large for the time. Sadly, when times got hard they were unable to maintain sales of such a quality product, and the firm faded away early in the Depression.

Kenton started making cast-iron automotive toys in 1903. It painted them red and coined the catchy name Red Devils for them. How devilish one of the early items looked, a clockwork automobile with tiller steering and a driver in a top hat, is open to question. Another early toy, dating from 1905, is a Runabout 13cm (5in) long. Dating from 1910 is an Open Touring Car, a model of an air-cooled Franklin, 21cm (8½in) long, complete with a driver and a lady passenger sitting in the back. Also from 1910 is a Boat-Tailed Speedster 18cm (7in) long. Quite a few of Kenton toys, including fire pumpers, are fitted with a driver. As the decades passed, the toys got larger, but they were still relatively simple coarse castings (compared with those of Dent) and, perhaps because of this, Kenton was still producing cast-iron vehicles into the late 1930s.

A number of other manufacturers made toys in the early days. Most fall into the 'unknown' category since they are not identified in the catalogues, but Grey Iron of Mount Joy, Pennsylvania is known to have made a selection of very small toys, a mere 4cm (1½in) long, alongside the soldiers which were their principal line.

Diecast toys made their first appearance in around 1910, though the technique of pressure diecasting was not to be fully exploited until the post-Depression 1930s. Dowst, which had developed the very latest in linotype printing machines, turned the skill of casting lead type to making small toys, novelties that it produced by the gross. It was only later that the business adopted the famous brand name Tootsietoy. Parallel development was going on in France, where several firms made small intricate pieces from lead hardened with antimony and tin, often with a bronzed finish. Most of the vehicles, like open tourers – usually made up of only one or two castings fitted with axles and tiny spoked wheels – are unmarked. However, SR (Simon & Rivollet) often did mark its toys. It is likely that there was cross-fertilization between Dowst and SR, perhaps with SR dies exported to America. The French products were often referred to as Pennytoys, as they were sold for a penny (or a few cents) on the streets of Europe.

EUROPEAN MANUFACTURERS:
LEHMANN

The easiest European toys to recognize from the end of the nineteenth century and the beginning of the twentieth were made by Lehmann. In addition to being brightly coloured and prominently marked – with a tinplate press that looks like a bell or with the initials EPL – they all have a clever and amusing action. Ernst Paul Lehmann, the genius behind these toys, became a partner in the failing firm of G. L. Eichner & Sons of Nuremberg in 1881. When Eichner died three years later, Lehmann changed the name of the business and continued alone, building up one of the pre-eminent and most prolific firms in his field. The toys were aimed at a mass market. With their bright colours, they had instant eye-appeal. Prices were kept low by the use of a newly developed, thin, cheap tinplate, some of which was actually manufactured in Wales. The clockwork action that propelled the toy along also captured the attention with one or another amusing gimmicks, such as a mule bucking between the traces of a cart or a sedan chair being pushed by a walking man. The calls of street traders would attract passers-by to watch these toys in action, and the comic effect would often produce a sale.

When automobiles appeared on the streets, Lehmann, who disliked this modern invention, nevertheless took advantage of the new range of moving prototypes. As early as 1897, he introduced to the mass market the Motor Car, a short horseless carriage with a driver out in front. The clockwork mechanism is concealed in the back of the carriage, and when the steering rod held in the driver's hand is pushed down one of the holes in the underframe, the steering can be set to go straight forward or describe left- or right-hand circles. This may not sound very

above: *The Bing 'Platform' Fire Escape was aimed at the US market (tinplate, 25cm/10in, c1910, Germany).*

exciting today, but in the late 1890s it had considerable novelty appeal.

Lehmann sold eighty-five per cent of his product through wholesalers spread across the world. Indeed, the box for the Motor Car has two sets of instructions on the lid, one in German and one in English. Lehmann was very conscious that the world's markets differed, so in 1904 he set out on a trip to promote his toys at the Louisiana Purchase Exposition at St Louis, Missouri. He and his party then went by rail to San Francisco.

He had just made an automotive toy that he might have targeted at the American market, which had fallen in a big way for comic strips and was eagerly buying toys based on comic-strip characters. Tut-Tut, a car with a coalscuttle-shaped bonnet, driven by an oversized driver who raised a horn to his lips and tooted down it, was not inspired by a comic strip, but it was such a caricature of a well-fed, self-aggrandizing capitalist that it could have been. Several Lehmann vehicles were available in different liveries and some were obviously targeted at overseas markets; the Aut Lala delivery van of 1907, for example, was decorated in Royal Mail livery and aimed at the British market. There was an open-top double-decker bus, as well as a variety of cars and vans with odd but memorable names that transcended frontiers – Uhu, Aha, Lolo, Oho – all derived from ritual greetings and toasts made at a humorous club of which Lehmann was a member.

Once a toy was put into manufacture, it stayed in for

center: *A restored early example of the Günthermann Vis-à-Vis Motor Car (painted tinplate, c1898, Germany).*

many years, and from 1910 Lehmann paid attention to covering his mechanisms with patents, first in Europe and then in America. One late-production taxi decorated in yellow-and-black Yellow Cab livery is marked PATD 2 DEC 1913 and USA 25 JAN 1927 on the chassis side. The 1912 Sears Roebuck catalogue made a feature of 'Lehmann's Reliable Mechanical Toys' and illustrated the Tut-Tut, the Naughty Boy, a truck and a bus. The pre-eminence of Lehmann over other manufacturers – Bing, Hess and Carette – also featured in the Sears catalogue is indicated by the fact that Lehmann is usually named, unlike the others. Lehmann must have contributed most of the German tinplate wind-ups that by this time had secured forty per cent of the American market.

BING

The year 1881 was a good one for the German toy industry, as Bing also turned to toy making. It covered all types of toys: stationary steam engines, trains, boats, optical and electrical toys with automotive subjects making up but a small part of the range. However, Bing commanded the quality end of the market,

and it made many of the better-looking larger toys in the Sears Roebuck catalogues from 1910. Bing sold only to retailers. Its 1906 catalogue gives an indication of the large size of the firm, which had about 3,000 employees and showrooms not only in Hamburg and Berlin, but also in London, Paris, Milan and Amsterdam. By 1914, Bing had no fewer than 5,000 workers.

No doubt Arthur Walter Gamage, who had started a shop in 1878 in Holborn, visited the Bing showroom in London to choose products to feature in his wonderful emporium and mail-order catalogues. His 1906 catalogue has three pages of mainly German motor cars, open-top buses and fire engines. Most of the lithographed illustrations are not labelled with the manufacturer, but some small ones have the Günthermann shield in one corner. The pride of the group, however, is from Bing and is described thus:

Model of Modern Motor Car. Very elegantly finished with extra strong, best quality clockwork, pneumatic rubber tyres, plastic seats (imitation cushions), cooling box in fine brass finish, and brake. Front axle adjustable to run straight or in a circle, with lanterns. Very elegant finish, with finely nickelled headlight for real burning.

featured advertisements for those quintessential English foods, Bovril and Grape Nuts. A slightly later French catalogue has the same two buses, but here they are operated by a German company, Grosse Omnibus Gesellschaft, advertising Suchard chocolate.

Bing also catered to the American market, and soon available, among other products, was an 'American "Platform" Fire-Escape with Motor Car'. This complex toy was described as being 'finely japanned, with strong clockwork, with winch to raise or lower the platforms, with hooter sounding "Tuff Tuff" pneumatic rubber tyres, front axle to adjust for straight or circular run, with two firemen.'

above: *A Günthermann Open Tourer with its driver and three passengers (tinplate, 20cm / 8in, c1910, Germany).*

The accompanying illustration has, in the corner, the initials GBN, standing for Gebrüder Bing Nürnberg (Bing Brothers, Nuremberg). The plates for the illustrations were supplied by the manufacturers and the Bing toys appear identically in its own 1906 catalogue. Gamage must have been an extremely important customer, buying in bulk, because the price he quoted was about a third less than Bing's list price! The importance of the British market is acknowledged by the manufacture of two 'Clockwork Omnibuses (London Street Car) Original English Model'. They were both run by the General Omnibus Company Limited and

Bing's automotive toys were often fitted with figures, especially drivers, and the firm sold separately three sizes of composition 'Motor Car Figures', all dressed with cloth. The cars often had brass lamps, some of which could be lit. There were opening doors on some toys, and glass windscreens were common. Handbrakes operated on a rear wheel. On some of the toys, the clockwork could be set to steer the car through more interesting patterns than the usual circles. These 'Running Figures' varied from triangular and figure-of-eight shapes to a much more complex six-petal daisy pattern.

GÜNTHERMANN

The trademark AWSG in an encircled shield was lithographed on to many of the toys produced by Günthermann, which released its first horseless carriage, complete with driver, in 1898. The initials SG were those of the founder of the firm, who had died some time before, and AW those of his factory manager, who had married the former's widow. After the latter's death in 1919, his initials were removed. One of the most photographed of Günthermann's early toys suggests an 1890s Peugeot *vis-à-vis*: a small open vehicle with a wheel at each corner, a high seat for the driver between the rear wheels and a passenger seat facing him. The driver grasps the wheel fixed to a column that projects vertically upwards between his knees, so the conveyance is conveniently neither left- nor right-hand drive. The driver would have had to peer around the passenger to see where he was going! The bodywork is nicely lithographed in bright colours on the exterior, with detail of the seat padding and kick panels in shades of fawn and brown. The large spoked wheels are fitted with solid white rubber tyres and there are lamps at the front. The driver is a particularly rounded model in painted tinplate. The apparent commonness of this sturdy toy can be partly accounted for by Günthermann's practice of making the same vehicle in a variety of sizes, the largest of this type being almost 30cm (12in) long.

Automobile racing began almost as soon as there were two vehicles available to compete, and before long specialist cars were designed to take part in a series of races sponsored by Gordon Bennett. Günthermann produced one toy in two different sizes; lithographed in white with gold detail with 'Coupe Gordon Bennett' up the sides of the long raked bonnet, it was driven by a leather-clad driver while a mechanic crouched sinisterly behind the scuttle. This

below: *A Bub Four-Light Limousine with chauffeur and opening rear doors (tinplate, 26cm/10in, c1912, Germany).*

is an early example of a manufacturer identifying a popular craze and then producing several colour variations to maximize sales. Günthermann was a prolific manufacturer, and it made small, cheaper vehicles in a variety of sizes – 12, 14, 16cm (4¾, 5½, 6⅓in) for instance – the cheapest having solid tin wheels and costing only a few pence (or cents).

HESS

An automotive toy by Hess is very easy to recognize, even from the black-and-white line illustrations in mail-order catalogues, because of the presence of a starting handle. These toys are often of generic racing cars with half-rounded drivers and left- and right-hand pieces of lithographed tin clipped together with tabs, then tabbed into the neatly decorated vehicle. There is an economy in the pieces that gives an air of solidity to the figure. Toy production at Hess started just before the turn of the century with a horseless carriage, and continued through trucks fitted with plaster drivers to the overall lithographed decoration of the cheap popular racers. The distinguishing feature of Hess – the over-sized, sleeved starting handle – juts out of the centre of the radiator, just below the word *Hessmobil*. This patented feature is the mechanism for winding up the flywheel of the friction drive. As time passed, the colours of the toys that remained in production became more garish and the quality declined, which meant that once the world depression began, the firm was not in a good enough condition to survive.

CARETTE

'This Trade Mark is a guarantee of superior workmanship.' So states the 1910 Carette catalogue. The trademark is a cog wheel with a steam regulator superimposed and initialled G C Co. N. It shows that the Frenchman Georges Carette had set himself up in Nuremberg in 1886 primarily to make steam models: trains, ships, stationary engines, and so on. Automobile production was but a very small part of his whole enterprise. What set his product apart, however, were the quality, flair and finesse that make the toys so desirable now. In common with other manufacturers, his vehicles were often made in a variety of sizes: a 1905 clockwork motor car came in three sizes – 19, 26 and 32cm (7½, 10½ and 13in) long – and with minute attention to detail, the passengers were available in three sizes, too. These early products were painted and varnished, or 'highly japanned', as the catalogue terms the finish.

A small proportion of their automotive toys were steam-driven, as were the vehicles on which they were modelled, and these went on being manufactured after the internal combustion engine had ousted steam. In 1910, a steam-powered 30cm (12in)-long Motor Bus was available, and the same pressings were also fitted with a clockwork motor. One version was called an 'Exact model of the London Motor Bus', the side adverts being for those non-British products Heinz 57 Varieties Sauces and Relishes and Van Houten's Cocoa. An accessory for the bus was a set of twenty-four figures: twenty-two ladies and gentlemen in a variety of outfits and hats, with

above: *A rare Open Tourer with folding fabric hood made by Pinard. Unfortunately, the windscreen is missing (tinplate, 28cm/11in, c1905, France).*

a driver and a conductor. There were other, papier-mâché figures for the cars, the best-quality lady having a motor veil.

The cheaper toys – and Carette did make simple spring- or flywheel-driven small toys that could compete in price with Lehmann and others – and the smaller versions of their other vehicles were lithographed to a very high standard of finish, which was most resistant to scratches and did not fade. The larger, deluxe toys were hand-painted and lined and then japanned. These 'parlour toys' represent the classiest examples of pre-World War I production, and just as many children would have given anything for one then, so would many collectors now.

The most exquisite 40cm (16in) -long Carette limousine could only be afforded by the wealthy. It was painted in aristocratic colours, such as rich maroon or opulent cream, with the roof and carriage lining in complementary colours. The spoked wheels were fitted with white rubber tyres and the roof sported a wire-framed luggage rack. The barrel-shaped headlamps and the squared carriage lamps on either side of the windscreen were of brass or nickel plate. The driver looked through a bevelled glass windscreen, and the passenger compartment,

with its opening doors, was likewise fully glazed. The loving care with which these scarce toys were treated is clear from the survival of several in very fine condition. Roof luggage racks, folding leather hoods, steering and fine detail occur further down the range too, but the Carette limousines can usually be distinguished from similar competing products by their distinctive lamps and bevelled glass.

In 1914 the Frenchman Carette had to flee Germany and the firm closed in 1917. The pressings were taken over by Karl Bub, who had been in business for many years but probably began making toy automobiles only in about 1912. Because of the lack of catalogues, it is difficult to

below left: *A Carette Tourer.* **centre:** *A Carette Limousine.* **right:** *A Bing Open Tourer. All were made in Germany.*

know exactly what the firm made, but the pieces were similar to those of the other German manufacturers and of good quality. Other famous European names were in business but were more significant in subsequent years.

The biggest type of toy car has always been the pedal car. It did not catch on very quickly in Europe, though there are simple home-made or exquisite one-off coach-built examples. But by 1911, Bon Marché in Paris was selling varying sizes of a racing car based on the current Grand Prix Peugeot. At the other end of the scale, tinplate Pennytoys, designed to be sold for one penny (sterling) or an equivalent small sum in other currencies, were available in great proliferation. Rossignol in

France began by making simple spirit-painted vehicles, while Meier, Distler, and Fischer (which made toys in two or more sizes), along with some of the other German manufacturers, utilized lithographed tin. Horseless carriages, automobiles, buses, fire engines and ambulances were made in abundance over the years, many of which are difficult to attribute because of the lack of a trademark. Despite the prodigious numbers that were made, their fragility meant that few survived.

During the early years of the twentieth century, American manufacturers' associations, such as the Toy Manufacturers of the USA (whose logo was Uncle Sam's top hat filled with toys), attempted to keep European product out and promote American product. Despite their efforts, by 1914 Germany was supplying about one-third of the goods on the market. Then a dramatically effective brake was applied to the importation of toys from Germany, for at the outbreak of the World War I and an embargo was placed on all German goods.

SOPHISTICATION, DIVERSIFICATION
AND DEPRESSION

In 1910, Henry Ford announced that automobile production would be standardized. The new Model T was to be the only model that his factories would produce, though it would be available in several body styles: car, truck, pick-up, and so on. A total of fifteen million Model Ts were made, so it is safe to say that a considerable number of the seven million cars that were on the American roads in 1918 were Model Ts. Although toys are supposed to mirror reality, you would not think so to look at the pages of the 1919 Sears Roebuck catalogue.

There was a page headed 'Strauss Reliable Mechanical Toys', which illustrated toys that are obviously derived from the ideas and techniques of Lehmann. Few are automotive, but there is a Trick Auto that goes forwards, backwards and in circles – not much of a trick – a Dandy

below: *The Märklin Road Engineer's Steam Roller and Trailer (48cm/19in, c1929, Germany).*

Roadster with a driver and mechanism, and a Boy-on-a-Delivery Mechanical Motorcyle. The various members of the Dayton Group were still active and producing their *new* distinctive friction toys, 'an American invention'. There is an open-cab, Buick-style limousine 33cm (13in) long and a similar delivery wagon 26cm (10½in) long, but the former was available in 1914 and the latter probably was too. A group of three sheet-steel, friction-powered commercials – a truck with barrels, a fire engine and a hook-and-ladder truck – range in size from 33cm to 48cm (13–19½in) and are of a familiar design. Light-gauge sheet steel has been used for several smaller vehicles, some of which look prewar. Others have very simplified but more up-to-date features, including opening doors and keys fastened to the clockwork spring. Two little tin vans made by A. C. Gilbert (of later Erector Set fame) feature US Mail and Ambulance lithography. They are pretty but primitive, and also of prewar origin. The reappearance of these items, however,

means that the industry was beginning to get back to normal production.

LUXURY TOYS

The Sears catalogue has new product, too. An attractive-looking but generic friction-steel roadster complete with driver provides the basis for a war-inspired Armored Auto, with a dummy gun and side fenders! There is also an Armored Tank with friction motor 30cm (12in) long. Heralding a line of toys that were, and still are, particularly popular in the US with its vast agricultural areas, the catalogue features:

above: *A pull-along American Railway Express Truck for sale in the 1928 Butler Bros catalogue (pressed steel, 66cm/26in, c1928, USA).*

A Dandy Miniature Farm Tractor Outfit. A mechanical miniature tractor which resembles a real farm tractor. Rear wheels are 5 inches in diameter and the front are 2⅞ inches. Made of sheet steel and iron, nicely painted. A good clockwork motor with lever attached to start and stop it at will. Complete with three miniature farm implements – wooden roller, 4¾ inches long, with two metal strips for attaching to tractor; a 5-inch metal disc harrow, and a double plow, size over all 10 x 4¼ inches including metal strips for attaching. Size of tractor by itself, over all, 9½in. long, 5¼in. wide, 5⅓in. high. Shpg. wt., 4¼lbs. $4.67.

The high cost of the entire outfit indicates that the American economy was picking up and that there was a sale for luxury toys. The same 1919 Sears Roebuck catalogue advertises a yet even more expensive toy, the Structo Auto Builder:

Boys, build your own mechanical auto. A valuable educational toy for the boy. A mechanically accurate toy automobile can be made from this outfit. Outfit consists of necessary parts to build a real toy mechanical automobile. Body made of medium grade sheet steel. Nicely finished. All other parts are made of metal and fit perfectly when they are assembled. Strong wheels 2½ inches in diameter and a strong clockwork motor to run auto. Fender and running board for each side about 1 inch wide. Instructive and very interesting for boys. Something new in the line of construction toys. Complete with small wrench, screwdriver and booklet of instructions for building. $5.98.

This model is 38.5cm (15in) long and bears a remarkable resemblance to the contemporary Stutz Bearcat Roadster, which was itself one of the many two-seat, long, round-tailed roadsters of the period. A further likeness is that the fully detailed gearbox is integral with the rear axle. Structo, whose slogan was 'Make Men of Boys', went on to produce many ready-made toys – trucks, vans, a Whippet Tank, fire engines, and so on. Many did not include clockwork or the expensive gear and transmission train, so they were much cheaper. A 1929 advert claimed that 'Heavier gauge steel is used than in any similar toy of comparable size', a claim that was probably true, because most steel toys of the same or heavier gauge were larger.

PRESSED-STEEL TOYS

The development of pressed-steel toys – sturdy and indestructible, as so many of the names suggest – was the major American manufacturing story of the 1920s. The technology was there in abundance. The materials and techniques that were used on the real auto only needed scaling down to large toy size, and an auto pressings subcontractor could even out the peaks and troughs in his mainstream production by making toys. The machinery was readily available, so firms that had been in the toy business could adapt to the popular new lines. The country was also embracing protectionism, and in 1922 import duties were increased to its highest-ever level, giving the new industries an important price cushion.

Black of Dayton Toys, one of the existing firms, and Miller set up Republic Floor Toys in the early 1920s. Building on their long experience, they sought a patent for a cover to protect friction motors from dirt and moisture, which meant that their range of smallish, 30 to 32cm (12–12¾in)-long steel cars and trucks could be played with outside in the yard. Still distinctly toylike, their all-in-one running boards, shaped like a flat-bottomed V, show their Dayton heritage. A large bus at 70cm (28in) and a slightly smaller ladder truck were closer to reality, but did not give the firm enough market penetration to survive beyond the graveyard year of 1932.

Making beautiful and action-packed toys assured of good sales to the rich, white sector of society while the economy was booming. Sturditoy, made by the Sturdy Corporation of Pawtucket, Rhode Island, conveniently located near its rich customers, flourished during the 1920s, only to disappear about 1933. Its advert in *Playthings* for 1927 claims: 'There's no substitute for Sturditoy. The final word in sheet steel toys. Oversize, overstrong & overwhelming favorites in the fine toy field.' The fifteen or so models were large, at 65 to 70cm (26–8in), and beautiful: open coal and dairy trucks, an armoured car, police patrol, steam shovel, US

above: *A Structo Roadster with a clockwork motor with a winding handle (pressed steel, 38cm/15in, c1921, USA).*

Mail truck, chemical pumper and even a travelling store, with cartons of nationally known products. The most spectacular pair was an American La France Water Tower with working pump action and a companion Fire Engine with hosereel. It must have been fun driving those round the yard, filling them with water and racing to put out a cardboard-box fire.

Kelmet, Keystone and Kingsbury sound like a firm of lawyers, but as toy manufacturers their only common feature (apart from their initial letter) is their use of pressed steel. Kelmet was short-lived, but it was significant in that some of its toys were models of actual trucks – White trucks in this case. Keystone, 'Toys That Last', secured the rights to Packard and, at the end of the 1920s, made a 60cm (24in) tipping truck from hefty 18-gauge steel that could hold 135kg (300lb) – and the factory paid the postage! The 1928 Butler Bros catalogue gives a full page to its large-size, pull-along toys, with a drawing of a portly gent, watch-

below: *A Kingsbury Sunbeam World Land Speed Record Car (pressed steel, 1927, USA).*

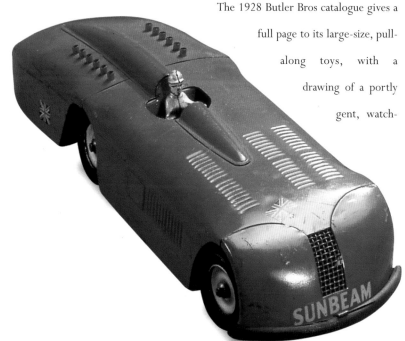

chain across his waistcoat, standing in the back of a truck, accompanied by the slogan 'trucks will support 200 pounds'. The Butler range consists of vans, police patrols, tankers, wreckers, and so on. One truck, claimed to be able to lift 200lb, is a 'Hydraulic dump truck 27 x 10¼ x 8, black, balloon type rubber tyres, steering front wheels, brass compress air tank (pressure produced by turning front crank), body automatically lowered by pressing lever.' But their Big Three, top-of-the-range, are a Water Pumper Fire Engine, an Aerial Ladder Truck and a Water Pumper Tower, which – to outdo competitors – not only has a klaxon horn, but 'shoots water 25 to 35 ft'. Handy if you had accidentally set fire to the chicken house! Keystone survived until 1958 by changing its manufacturing material to wood during World War II and to plastic thereafter.

KINGSBURY

Kingsbury, whose most important manufacturing decade was the 1930s, made many vehicles that were models of the real thing and not just generic examples. The firm's antecedents go back to before the turn of the century. Its strong toys, some made out of medium-gauge steel, were frequently powered by clockwork. Kingsbury's product during the 1920s was the usual stuff – trucks, vans, dump trucks – with a considerable emphasis on fire engines of several sorts, including ones that were a match for the top of the Sturditoy and Keystone ranges. Their good clockwork, and their insight into what would capture the public's imagination, put a new type of automobile into the range.

Speed-record mania hit the world in the late 1920s and the US, with its good supply of long beaches, salt flats and other suitable stretches of firm ground became the host for many attempts on the record. This came at a good time for Kingsbury. Its production stocks were building up as the post-World War boom lost momentum and the toy market decreased across the country. What was needed was a new product to boost the sales, and the company found it in toys representing the high-speed automobiles. The big red Sunbeam 'slug' of 1927, powered by a clockwork motor to race across the dirt in the yard (just like the full-size one at Daytona), and fitted with rubber tyres vulcanized directly on to the hubs for straighter running, was a brand-new idea. It was not a racing car, but a large, satisfying, brilliantly coloured record car. This was just the thing to create envy among schoolmates

and an upsurge in sales. Bluebird II, with its square radiators located prominently on each side above the rear wheels, followed in 1928. The Sunbeam Golden Arrow of 1929 – long, low, corrugated and golden – looked like no other vehicle made before and could hardly have been more different from the high-axle Model T. Kingsbury made its models 50cm (20in) long and gained fame among collectors by creating one of the most recognizable of toy vehicles. The company survived the Depression on the back of such an innovative product.

BUDDY L

There is one name from the 1920s that has done more than merely survive until today. Buddy L is flourishing in the 1990s, with the latest steel and plastic scale-model, electronically controlled, light and sound vehicles. The current fire pumpers sound ear-splittingly like the real thing. The name Buddy L (which has been styled with quotes or a hyphen over the years) came from that of Buddy, the son of Fred Lundahl,

left: A Kingsbury Bluebird World Speed Record Car (painted steel, 1929, USA).

below: Kingsbury Golden Arrow World Land Speed Record Car (pressed steel, c1930, USA).

above: The excellent International Coach manufactured by Buddy L (74cm/29in, c1927, USA).

who was called 'Buddy L' to distinguish him from the other Buddys in the neighbourhood.

The Moline Pressed Steel Company had been in business since before World War I, and in 1921 the firm contracted to make parts for International trucks for International Harvester, which, suffering a hiatus in its business, suspended the deal. Lundahl, who had already made sturdy automotive toys for his son, turned his inventive mind to them as an alternative product. He took a sample to F. A. O. Schwartz, who was mightily impressed by Lundahl's toys and salesmanship and ordered 500 of them. The factory turned out 4,000 pieces in the first year. At the 1922 New York Toy Fair, Lundahl exhibited an Express Truck, a Dump Truck, a Steam Shovel and Ford Model Ts – at last a pressed-steel group of Model Ts. There was an impressive increase in production up to 1925, when 200,000 items left the factory.

These toys were in a class of their own. They were made of thicker steel (22-gauge to the others' 28-gauge), with the cowl and body riveted together and spot-welded on to the chassis and with a fully working steering wheel. These realistic

indestructible toys worked very well. They were big, 60 to 90cm (24–36in) long and strong enough to be sat on and scooted along with the feet. You could kneel on the open-truck body, with one hand on the bonnet or mudguard and the other on the steering wheel, pushing with your free foot. It became common to supply them fitted with a removable bicycle or tractor-like seat. Their prices were high – in the same range as Structo sets – but they were cheaper than pedal cars; there was nothing else like them, and the economy was booming. Lundahl did not lose his ties with International Harvester when he went into toy production; indeed, he made the Red Baby truck for them to sell as a 'part' from their catalogue.

The Buddy L factory was expanded, and in 1926 it made a non-automotive concrete mixer that could actually mix concrete 'Just like the Big Ones'. The pride of the early range was undoubtedly a 1927 model of an International Coach, 75cm (30in) long and weighing 7.5kg (16½lb). The same year, a colour advertising leaflet devised by Lundahl, *The Story of Buddy L*, promoted the range; 1928 saw the production of a Trench Digger that could dig scale trenches. The 1930 retail price list featured ten trucks, four fire vehicles, eight pieces of construction equipment, a cheaper Junior Line, a selection of Fords, and a similar quantity of railroad items. The firm was going from strength to strength. Meanwhile, disastrously, the Wall Street market crash in late 1929 precipitated the world economy into a major recession. By 1933, fourteen million people were out of work, industrial production was half that of 1929, and only twenty Buddy L toys, a quarter of the 1930 list, were in production.

OTHER AMERICAN MANUFACTURERS

The heavier gauges of pressed steel that toy makers used were equally suitable for the larger, child-carrying pedal cars. The Sears Roebuck 1919 catalogue shows a selection, from 'Low Priced' ($6, exactly the price of the Structo set) steel and wood toys that were small and basic (frame, seat, bonnet, steering wheel, wheels and pedals), through 'Medium Priced' (similar, but with windscreen and a trunk on the rear) to 'Crackerjack Value' (similar-looking but mainly steel). Unfortunately most of these and an all-steel type were unmailable; unless you lived near a railroad station, they were very difficult to obtain.

American National Automobiles of Toledo, Ohio, and Steelcraft of Murray, Ohio, both made steel toys and pedal cars during the 1920s and early 1930s. American National Automobiles made a great range of pedal cars – 'The premier line...exactly modelled after the real cars...lustrous enamel finishes in flashy color combinations. Each with adjustable

pedals' – from a very cheap basic Whippet to a Marmon and a Studebaker. The listed equipment improved as you went up the range, from: 'cast steering wheel, gas lever, motor meter and pedals', through: 'composition steering wheel, gas lever, horn, instrument board, adjustable windshield, nickeled motor-meter, metal headlights, license plate, gear shift, rubber pedals, oil can, oil' to 'composition steering rod, gas lever, French horn, instrument board, nickeled adjustable windshield, spotlight, nickeled motor-meter, metal lamps, license plate, gear shift, stationary hood, round bumper, "die-form" fenders, rubber pedals, motor buzzer, oil can, oil'.

In their general range, Steelcraft made GMC trucks in the mid-1920s and added the distinctive Mack bulldog cab later. They made a Mack pedal dump truck, suitable for three- to six-year-olds; a Model T Roadster, for two- to five-year-olds; and a Dodge Runabout, for three- to seven-year-olds. Big brothers, or rich kids, could have a Chrysler Roadster: 'Very sporty, isn't it? Bullet-shaped headlights, spotlight, real rubber tires and all the fancy trim. A real car for you. Length, 50½ inches overall. $31.50.' Surviving the Depression, Steelcraft made up-to-date models, including an Airflow Dump Truck. Their later production included a Pedal Racer and a Lincoln Zephyr pedal car in 1941.

After 1914 there was a gap in the market brought on by the embargo on the import of German toys. Apart from Strauss and A. C. Gilbert, there were virtually no experienced American manufacturers of cheap, bright, attractive, lithographed tinplate toys – and even Strauss does not seem to have been in operation around 1920. Chein (pronounced *Chain*) had been in business in Harrison, New Jersey, since the turn of the century, and in 1925 began producing a series of a Mack bulldog trucks, many decorated with excellent lithography in clear, bright colours. There were fourteen different versions, ranging in size from 40 to 75cm (17–30in). A number of these were simple tippers or wreckers – others, such as the orange Hercules Ready-Mixed Concrete barrel truck, have a very high 'desirability factor' among collectors. They are fitted with lithographed wheels, with the white tyres marked 'Hercules USA Chein T. M.', so for once there is no difficulty in identifying the maker. They also made generic square-bonnet trucks and buses, including a beautiful Royal Blue Lines Pullman Bus. The range continued until the mid-1930s, and the firm remained in business making toys until 1979.

Girard is a name that keeps cropping up as a manufacturer of a wide variety of tinplate mechanical toys, but little is known about the history of this firm. Not all of its toys were marked with a name, and they do not seem to have survived well. Other litho tinplate manufacturers, such as Wolverine and Lindstrom, appeared at the tail end of this postwar period; toys from the latter company became important as advertising vehicles, carrying ads for Life Savers, varieties of biscuits, and so on. But the main story at this time is that of the prodigious rise of Marx.

MARX

Louis Marx was employed by Ferdinand Strauss around the beginning of World War I and was soon running the factory. After they fell out, Marx set up his own business, buying an existing toy plant in Erie, Pennsylvania. At some time he also acquired dies from Strauss and Girard. These are the bare bones of the moves Marx made for strategic or tactical reasons. This genius, who had an instinct for what would be popular, created new product with aplomb, borrowed ideas without too obviously plagiarizing (where borrowing was appropriate), ruthlessly broke into markets, kept his firm going through depression and war and established factories worldwide, becoming in the 1950s the world's biggest toy maker. He sold out in 1972 at the age of seventy-six.

'Mechanical Toys That Are Durable and Mechanically Perfect' was the Marx slogan, but what drove him was the conviction that he needed to make better toys for less money. He was not above investigating competitors' products, pricing structures and manufacturing sources, both in America and Europe, in his attempt to do just that. A successful product was not one that was merely cheaper than the competition, but one that appealed to the purchaser – both adult and child. Six qualities were needed, Marx stated: familiarity, surprise, skill, play value, comprehensibility and sturdiness. Given the appeal novelty action toys had in the US, this might seem to be a fairly obvious set of criteria, but the important thing is that they were laid down and on the whole adhered to, keeping the firm on a consistently successful track. The name was kept in the public eye by printing – on the outside of the toy, not hidden underneath – the distinctive trademark. Even at a quick glance, the X of Marx inside a circle stands out.

The most distinctive and memorable group of Marx toys were the Crazy (or Funny) Cars. The Funny Flivver of 1926, with its pivoting front wheels and rotating driver's head, was the simple beginning of a style that lasted up to 1941. These cars were lithographed tin wind-ups fitted with integral drivers, with larger wheels at the rear and an eccentric action that caused the front wheels to turn in apparently random directions and the driver's head to rotate. As the years passed, the action became more complicated, so that the vehicles bucked about, 'causing' the figures to jump and shake. Such novelties were also applied to commercial vehicles. A fire engine with a fireman up a ladder worked on the same principle as the Funny Flivver. The best-known example from this era is the Joy Rider type, which came in many variations over subsequent years: 'Joy Riders Elope,' says a 1930 advert, complete with speed swirl drawings. 'His head's in a whirl – and his "girl friend" holds on for dear life! Backwards, forwards, around and around. They're getting nowhere fast.' The diminutive girl sits back-to-back

with the driver on the trunk, which actually looks like the piece of luggage and is the back-stop to prevent the vehicle from overbalancing backwards as it bucks and scoots around. All this you got for just 49 cents, including postage.

The college boy Old Jalopy type began with the Leaping Lizzie in about 1927. These Ford Model A-type 'old bangers' were run around campuses, their dents and rust patches covered with amusing remarks: 'Four wheels, no brakes; My Lizzie of the Valley; Hop Inn…' So popular was this toy that it was re-created during

below: *The Tri-ang Ford Royal Mail Van, made by Lines Bros, is marked with the early 'Triangtois' trademark (46cm/18in, c1933, UK).*

the 1950s. There was no limit to the variety of action toys. There was a four-piece tractor set with a guaranteed unbreakable Marx spring; an aluminium Tractor, which would climb over piles of books or sand; a series of Mack trucks made out of many pieces of tabbed and folded, prettily lithographed tin; a Stutz, large at 40cm/16in; a similar Fire Chief's Car with siren and bright and dim electric lights. The advert for the 'Motor Cycle Cop, Entirely new and different motor action in a modern looking motorcycle! Upsets to either right or left…rights itself…and then another upset! Surprising action!' has the explanation that the motor is geared to large side keys to make the toy automatically right itself. Then there were racing cars, bus stations, gas stations – virtually anything you could think of – and many non-automotive toys as well, all at competitive prices. That Marx was in really good shape to survive the Depression is indicated by the date of introduction of the Motor Cycle Cop – 1933.

The contrast between lithographed tin and cast iron was great, but the new style of toy by no means ousted the old. Williams continued producing a small Model T doctor's coupé and a good Fordson tractor. Meanwhile, Dent went on making its fine castings, few

right: *This Arcade Yellow Cab has a painted finish (18cm/7in, c1932, USA).*

of which were marked with the name but had clear, raised lettering, for example: 'Junior Supply Co. New York 1923 Philadelphia' cast on a Mack parcel truck. Kenton became known for its commercial vehicles, many of which have their names cast on the side: there is an OIL GAS tank truck; a CONTRACTORS' dump truck, a JAEGER cement mixer. Apart from the PICKWICK NITE COACH, a distinctive long-distance coach with its upper deck shorter than the lower, Dent's good ranges of double-decker buses, coaches and fire engines often have no markings. Over the years, the wheels varied from heavy-spoked wheels through solid discs to wooden hubs with white balloon tyres. The styles of the truck cabs kept up with those of full-size manufacturers, so rough introduction dates can be worked out.

ARCADE

Arcade became the most prolific American manufacturer, and most of its toys are marked inside the casting. The company had been in business since 1868 and changed its name to Arcade in 1884, though it did not make its mark in the production of automotive toys until the 1920s. Then it set about making deals with the full-size manufacturers, so that most of its products are models of actual vehicles, including Fords, Chevrolets, Mack trucks, Fordson tractors, and Fageol coaches. Moreover, it made exclusive deals with firms like Yellow Cab and produced special items for promotional giveaways, including a truck for Brinks and, later, a milk-bottle-shaped vehicle for Borden. 'Perfect pocket size reproductions of the "real ones" – sturdily built – no clockwork to get out of order.' Character merchandising, popular since the turn of the century, was exploited, too, with a good representation of the Andy Gump '348' car. The vehicles often came in two sizes, referred to in advertising simply as large or small, the sizes varying mainly between 12 and 32cm (5–13in). Commonly the finish was one single colour – often red, blue or grey – with the name Arcade applied to a door with a black and gold sticker. However, the Yellow Cab could be bought in yellow with a black top, or in yellow and red, brown and white, black and white or blue and white. The castings are well detailed and very neat, but usually not intricate, with only simple working parts such as tipping mechanisms.

Arcade does not fit too well the end-of-1933 chapter division that is used in this book, because of a very happy circumstance. In 1933, to combat the sense of desperation about the economic situation, Chicago mounted a grand exposition, the Chicago Century of Progress. Visitors were to be transported around by specially designed GMC articulated buses that were operated by Greyhound Lines. The dark blue, long-bonneted cabs pulled white trailers, and their windows were edged like scalloped blinds. They were decorated with the dark blue Greyhound trademark and the roofs carried an appropriate legend. Arcade made the official replicas for sale as souvenirs. They came in five sizes, ranging from 14 to 36cm (5½–15in) and were a raging success. So was the fair. It was held again in 1934, and once again Arcade produced the souvenirs. What a way to bridge the problem years! Many examples of these toys have survived.

Arcade continued to produce realistic models: the Ford Sedan of 1934 replaced the one that was produced in 1930, which had in turn replaced that of 1924; the wreckers and other trucks were updated with the new cab styles; white rubber tyres replaced the chromed cast wheels. Promotional and souvenir items remained a large part of Arcade's production, and they made even more groups of buses, including two sizes of Greyhound bus for the Great Lakes Exposition of 1936, three sizes of the 1939 New York World's Fair Bus and two versions of the same fair's Tractor-Train. A recent publication lists the 263 different Arcade toys in their variety of lengths.

HUBLEY AND KILGORE

Hubley, which was a cast iron manufacturer of very long standing, came to be Arcade's main direct competitor. It usually marked its toys, but many are in any case distinguishable by their complexity. Some consider that Hubley's 27cm (11in)-long 1927 Packard Straight 8 is the finest cast-iron toy ever produced. The long-bonneted, elegant model has front doors that open, a driver sitting on detailed seats and bonnet sides that open to reveal the engine. The scarcity of this toy is occasioned partly by its original high price, which caused it to be dropped from the catalogue as the recession began to bite, and partly because it was much more likely than other cast-iron toys to get damaged in play. Hubley's five-ton truck came complete with tools. The General steam shovels could be used to dig sand or dirt, which the Huber Road Roller – its complexity increasing through the five sizes – could then roll flat. There was also the Elgin roadsweeper, an excellent working model, which could sweep the road clean.

Produced, as was the real thing, after the economy began to recover, three sizes of Hubley's Chrysler Airflow toys had take-apart bodies, while a larger fourth size even had electric headlamps. Hubley had one area virtually to itself – motorcycles. Many of the toys authorized by the manufacturers are finely detailed, and the name Indian, Harley Davidson or whatever can be seen clearly written on the petrol tanks. The very accurate solo motorcycles, with sidecar or tricycle-type bikes, are fitted with riders – some integral, others detachable – portraying policemen, postmen, or civilians. Hubley proved to be among the most desirable of American toy makers.

One of several other smaller manufacturers that produced cast-iron toys and should not be forgotten is Kilgore. In business from 1920 to 1978, it made low-priced quality toys, but excelled in the late 1920s with a multi-piece Roadster – now considered to be a Pontiac – similar in size to Hubley's Packard. The body is separate from the chassis, and the radiator, bumpers, sidelight-cum-cowl-band, windscreen surround, and wheels are all chromed. Kilgore survived the recession by making small ten-cent toys with rubber wheels that challenged the up-and-coming diecasts of Tootsietoy. It also went up against Hubley with a small group of motorcycles. This most flexible company was arguably the first, in 1937, to use plastic (Bakelite) for small 10cm (4in) auto toys. When the firm closed, two much-photographed, nickel-plated showroom examples of a 1934 Ford V-8 Coupé and a Sedan were sold to a collector (the original toys were painted).

GERMAN MANUFACTURERS

When World War I ended in defeat for Germany, the country was in a sorry state: the government was weak; the reparations demanded drove it close to bankruptcy; and inflation raged. But Lehmann's production continued apace. Although part of Germany's market, America, in the main refused to buy their toys, though the rest of the world still wanted them. Lehmann had had the foresight to bill in the most stable currency, the

American dollar, and thus it had no difficulty defying inflation, because it was able to purchase raw materials at a competitive price. The bulk of the production was still novelty toys, but the style of the clockwork, lithographed tinplate automobiles was brought up to date, starting immediately with a curvaceous Terra town car. This was later released, as usual, in other named liveries, including a yellow and black taxi. The rest of the saloons were squarish and ranged from a thin tinplate Sedan at 14cm (5½in) to the quality electric-lighted Luxus at 32.5cm (13in), resplendent in cream and red, and its non-lighted companion, the Gala. There were garages suitable for the Sedan and the Galop racer. Very scarce now is the Deutsche Reichspost mail van, as is the delightful group of four motorbikes, which remain stable on two wheels by means of a gyroscope hidden within the frame cladding. These toys remained in the catalogue variably up to 1935 and 1940, neither Lehmann's death nor the rise of Hitler in the early 1930s affected their popularity.

The roll call of German toy manufacturers – Eberl, Bing, Bub, Distler, Doll, Fischer, Günthermann, Hess, Kellermann, Märklin, Tipp & Co., Oro (Orobr) – shows that although these firms did not find the going as smooth as Lehmann did, internal economic and political difficulties could be overcome by strong export products.

Bing found that its output had to change, from exclusive toys for the rich child to a cheaper product that more people could afford. Tinplate became thinner and the pressings were simplified, though opening rear doors remained a feature. Cheaper clockwork motors were used and steering was also simplified. The earlier complex patterns could no longer be created, but Bing dabbled with a remote steering system. Separate brass or nickel lamps were not fitted, though the top of the range had large, battery-powered electric light bulbs. Hand enamelling was no longer used, and even large, flat areas of colour were lithographed. Many of these changes paralleled the move to greater standardization in the full-size vehicles, typified by four versions, all 17.5cm (7in) long, of the Model T – all in black, of course. After Bing was bought by Bub in 1933,

below: *A Ford Model A Truck with the details of Arcade on the castings (cast iron, 15cm/6in, c1932, USA).*

CAPTAIN CAMPBE

OFFICIAL WORLD SPEED RECOR

right: *Sir Malcolm Campbell's World Land Speed Record Car, 'Bluebird'. The box shows the record speed as 245.73mph, though most books give it as 246.09mph (tinplate, 51cm/20in, c1931, Germany).*

BLUE

above: *The Doll & Cie Open Steam Wagon, no. 802, is driven by a single-cylinder steam engine found under the bonnet (51cm/20in, c1929, Germany).*

some of its models were still made under the original trademark.

Bub had already acquired Carette, and by the 1920s it was ready to go into mass production. With so much input from take-overs, Bub did not develop a strong house style, and it is mainly identifiable from the K. B. N. trademark and the relatively inexpensive, but classy-looking, lithographed tinplate wheels. A smart 30cm (12in) -long boxy saloon has wooden spoked wheels nicely represented on a solid disc of tin. In their extensive range, there was also a taxi that had been given a more up-market treatment than usual: a yellow cab complete with electric lights, steering and a driver. Günthermann also thrived in this era, making clockwork-powered saloon cars and tourers running on wheels with rubber tyres, but its most spectacular toys were speed-record cars. In common with Kingsbury, it made a Golden Arrow. Its Bluebird III has lithographed rivet detail. Kay Don's Silver Bullet was the

longest of the group at 56cm (22in). All of these Kingsbury and Günthermann toys were individually boxed, and the illustrations, some of which included pictures of the drivers, look as if they were officially approved. Another German firm, Tipp & Co. (Tippco) made toys, some of them on quite a large scale, in well-printed but much thinner-gauge tin. Around 1930, in an unaccustomed outburst of European frivolity, it made an open tourer for the Christmas market. Decorated with pictures of toys, it carried in the trunk a pine tree fitted with electric lights and was driven by an rather unhappy-looking Father Christmas.

FRENCH PRODUCTS

France suffered from its lack of an industrial centre. There were many small factories scattered in village locations, which made raw materials difficult to source and the finished product hard to distribute. Nevertheless, two toy firms – typically and patriotically making recognizable models of French vehicles – had been in business since before 1900. Charles Rossignol used his initials C.R. as his trademark and made his first model, a steam tram, in 1880. The first car, a Renault Taxi 17cm (7in) long, was produced in 1905, but the firm is famous for a range of buses made between 1923 and 1929. The single-decker Paris bus, with its windows and roof a distinctive cream and the lower part in green, was made by both De Dion and Renault, becoming more modern over the years (as the driver's cab was enclosed, and so on). Rossignol faithfully mirrored the changes, producing accurate models in several sizes finished with lovely lithography. Vans also featured in the catalogue, as did cars. In 1930 the company made a group of Renaults – sports, coupés and cabriolets – all with electric lights, opening doors and boot. The company even supplied a lithographed tin garage in which to park them. The firm was notable for making a much wider range of sizes than was usual, from Pennytoys to large floor toys.

JEP (Jouets en Paris) began life as SIF, then traded as J de P between 1928 and 1932, and it remained in business until 1965. Early product was poor and cheap, but as J de P the business became a quality toy maker, it produced Renault, Hotchkiss and Rochet Schneider cars about 28cm (11in) long. These were followed by even more impressive Renaults and some Bugattis. JEP also made larger-scale tinplate cars with accurate radiators – Hispano Suiza, Rolls-Royce, and so on. In those days of coach-building (apart from Renault, whose early cars had the distinctive 'coalscuttle' bonnet), it was mainly the radiator that distinguished the make. JEP also reproduced a typical body and mechanism, including prop shaft and differential, with studied realism, to complement the grilles.

Accuracy was epitomized by the legendary Alfa P2, manufactured by CIJ. This distinctive 53cm (21in) racing car, with its high, long bonnet and pointed tail, was made in thick tinplate and fitted with wire wheels with rubber tyres. The pressings are well shaped and fit together neatly. The steering worked and had a

below: *The Märklin Tractor uses a two-speed pulley mechanism (27cm/10.5in, c1929, Germany).*

powerful clockwork motor. Made for several years, it featured leaf-spring suspension, hinged filler caps, leather bonnet straps and a single-colour painted finish (red, blue, green). This was a very popular toy in many European countries, and it is puzzling that CIJ did not make anything else like it. Neither, mind you, did anyone else.

The range of scale cars is Jouets Citroën. The models were conceived as a marketing tool for the promotion of Citroën's full-size vehicles, but they were a phenomenal success as toys. They were first released in 1923, and 15,000 10cv Torpedoes were sold during the first year, prompting the release of a 5cv C3 cloverleaf in 1924, a delivery van and a B2 taxi in 1925, the new 10cv Torpedo in 1926 and the flat-bed lorry and coupé in 1927. André Citroën is quoted as saying: 'The child is our future client. His first

below: The Bub Four-light Limousine comes equipped with its own toolbox (tinplate, 30cm/12in, c1922, Germany).

three words must be Papa, Mama and…Citroën.' The pressings, with their realistically scaled roof, bonnet and boot curves, have a no-nonsense solidity that characterizes the full size and makes them the best model cars of the era. The enamelled finish mirrors the rich colours of the full-size vehicles. The C6 chassis, the most desirable of kits, comes complete with the correct dashboard, carburettor and electric lights, as well as the usual steering, suspension and transmission.

ITALIAN COMPANIES

The turmoil of a recently unified Italy led, in 1921, to the rise to power of Mussolini, and the resulting period of stability enabled a small toy industry to develop. Metalgraph, in industrial Milan, made its first car in 1920 and its last at the end of the 1930s, although it concentrated mainly on its industrial tinplate lithographed packaging, biscuit tins and the like. Its mid-1920s production – a coupé de ville, racers and a delivery van – were of average quality and no competition for the German toys. From about 1920, Ingap, located in Padua in the more prosperous north-east, used tin to make a very wide range of toys. The business thrived, expanding from just twenty employees in 1920 to around 600 by the beginning of World War II. Cardini's range included only five vehicles during the 1920s, but its all-metal, stove-enamelled, clockwork Fiat 18BL lorry is of excellent quality.

BRITISH MAKERS

Britain's lithographed tinplate manufacturers owe their skill to the industry that churned out well-printed and sometimes ingenious biscuit and chocolate tins – some in the shape of the firm's delivery vans. Other manufacturers owe the inspiration for their product to Bing and the other German firms. The tinplate was usually thin but well printed, and the clockwork was commonly a cheap coil spring. Whitanco is reputed to have made the first toy car in 1915, and by 1919 had made 1½

cab – an early open style and a subsequent closed one – with a series of different decorations: ambulance, Royal Mail and Carter Paterson Express Carriers, and the Stop Me and Buy One ice-cream van with a driver. Burnett made some delivery vans and a couple of Ubilda kits suitable for even the most ham-fisted child.

One of the most significant developments in British toy making took place in 1919. Three brothers broke away from their family company, which had been making toys and baby

million toys, though not all were vehicles. Despite their use of German tooling, competition from Europe forced the firm out of business by 1923. The survival rate of their fragile product is low. Brimtoy began production during the same period and may have been directly inspired by German product. They were taken over by A. Wells & Co., whose trademark consisted of country-style, roofed water wells, romantically labelled Wells o' London. Its 1931 catalogue illustrates vans with two types of

carriages, to set up Lines Bros Ltd, whose witty trademark is a triangle (a device made up of three lines). By 1925, their Merton factory on the outskirts of London was the most up-to-date, and they were producing pull-along wooden toys, some featuring moulded plywood, as well as making steel and wooden pedal cars and three-wheeled Fairycycles for younger children. There is also a shiny aluminium caterpillar

above: *These André Peugeot 201 Vans may have been promotional containers (tinplate, 15cm/6in, c1932, France).*

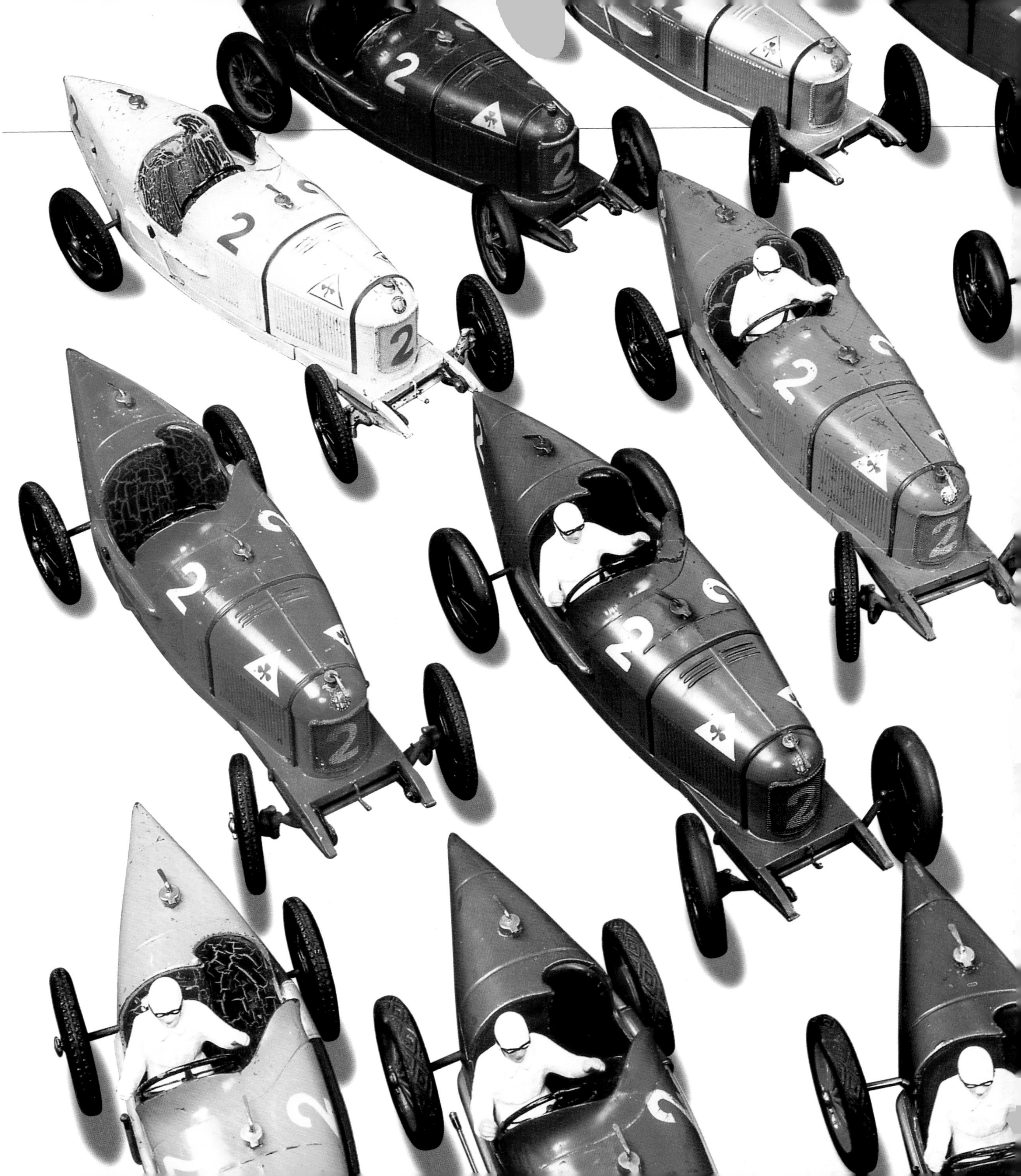

tractor that can climb over a pile of books that is similar to one made by Marx and makes one wonder which of these inventive firms conceived it and which 'borrowed' the idea.

At the beginning of the 1930s, Meccano — a company renowned for making constructional sets, with which a child could make anything from wheelbarrows to cranes and bridges — adopted the idea of making sets to create cars. Enough pieces were supplied to make a racing car with long tail and separate wings or a sports car with short tail and integral wings-cum-running-boards, and so on. There was not a great deal of flexibility, but the colours were vibrant and two sizes were made. If you could not build them yourself, you could buy the larger size already put together and one similar to the smaller size in a non-constructional version. They were all produced up to the end of the decade.

There was a smattering of accurate vehicles in unusual materials. Wallwork made two large and beautiful cast-iron buses — a single- and a double-decker. Ranlite experimented with Bakelite, one of the early plastics, producing two saloons and a Golden Arrow record car in 1931. These were expensive toys, but they did not cost as much as the most desirable European vehicles of all: accurate, large-scale pedal cars represented by the Citroën Clover Leaf and the Bugatti Grand Prix Type 52, both made by the manufacturers of the full-size vehicle; the one-off Le Mans Bentley; or Lines Bros' more representational fluted-bonnet Vauxhall.

far left: *These CIJ Alfa Romeo P2 racing cars come in many colours (pressed steel, 53cm/21in, 1933, France).*

above: *The Ranlite Austin Saloon with its petrol pump. An ingenious, if cumbersome, steering mechanism was available as an extra that allowed the child to guide the model while standing (bakelite/pressed steel, 26cm/10in, 1931, UK).*

above: *The Whitanco Open delivery Truck uses a clockwork motor (tinplate, 13cm/5in, c1920, UK).*

below: *This Two-Seater Sports Car was a departure for Meccano as it was sold only as a finished model (tinplate, 22cm/8.5in, c1934, UK).*

sophistication, diversification and depression

In America, the toy car production era of the 1930s did not start properly until 1933, when the newly elected President Roosevelt announced his New Deal programmes to rescue the country from the Depression. By then, many toy firms had gone out of business, and those that remained were running with a much-reduced volume at the cheaper end of their long-running production. The more complicated working cast-iron models with a multiplicity of pieces disappeared from the catalogues, and tinplate manufacturers used up scrap tin from a toy by lithographing the plain side with decoration for a different one.

Wyandotte All Metal Products had made a range of steel and wood trucks in several sizes during the 1920s, and in the 1930s it simplified its manufacture by exploiting the new American craze for streamlining. Depending on your taste, these pressed-steel toys look 'crude', 'somewhat unfinished' or have a '1930s' charm'. The automobiles and trucks were manufactured from as few pieces of material as possible, with as few machine and finishing operations as was feasible. Just as a soldier's steel helmet can be punched out of a sheet of metal between two shaped platens in a heavy press because all the elements spread out from the centre and there are no undercuts, so too can a toy auto or truck body. One tool might punch out the windows from a flat sheet, create the louvres and cut the metal to size; a second would draw the steel down from the roof to the swelling streamlined fenders. Then the truck's back could be cut and folded, the two pieces welded together and painted, and the wheels fixed on. Wyandotte was very good at producing the streamlined spatted fenders that distinguish its later toys, which were made very cheaply in vast quantities. A few of these toys are highly collectable. Wyandotte's circus trucks have

below: *The Tippco Double Deck Bus with adverts showing real products (tinplate, 26cm/10in, c1934, Germany).*

a lovely lithographed

tinplate back, and it is famed for its coffin-nosed Cord and its La Salle and Trailer set. Wyandotte survived World War II by making wooden toys and was bought by Marx in 1950.

Streamlined fairings over the wheels were not exclusive to one manufacturer, and Metalcraft used the style to update its range of solidly oblong, unsophisticated pressings. The original basic cab, with a long bonnet, square-peaked driver's compartment and mudguards-cum-running-boards, was based on the White truck, and the backs were used for advertising. A Coca-Cola truck had its rear shaped like a bottle carrier fitted with bottles, the H. J. Heinz Co. slatted-box back advertised Rice Flakes, spaghetti and tomato ketchup. The decoration compensated for the heavy metal, the thick paint and crude electric light fittings. The replacement streamlined cab, though it did not have electric lights, is visually a great improvement. The firm did stay solvent from 1927 through the Depression,

undergoing a product revamp in 1933, but failed in 1937.

WEATHERING THE DEPRESSION

Structo and Steelcraft were still in business throughout this period, as was Buddy L, but the latter was finding survival hard going. It held its prices so low in 1935 that it almost seemed as though it was having a going-out-of-business sale. Indeed, in 1936 it announced that 'No more will be made'. Paradoxically, the car design that rescued Buddy L was a disaster at full size. The four-light streamlined Scarab failed miserably in the market, but the

above: *An assortment of tinplate motorcycles by Tippco, Arnold and Mettoy.*

above: *A Metalcraft Heinz Delivery Truck with electric lights (pressed steel, 30cm/12in, c1934, USA).*

Buddy L toy, a small, squashed-looking single-piece body, available with or without clockwork motor, looking as little like the rest of the range as possible, sold thousands and thousands. Buddy L's heavy trucks had been updated in about 1933 with peaked cab roofs. Small changes to radiators and other parts were made each year. Later a prototypical International cab was introduced, and this was altered to follow the upgrades on the full-size vehicle. To make the range stand out on the toy-store shelf, the trucks were given distinctive, bright colour schemes. To start with the cab would be, say, yellow and the back of the truck red. In 1936, Buddy L had the idea of partially dipping the yellow cab in red paint so that a diagonal split was created, the line running from the top of the radiator to the bottom behind the doors. In 1941, when the cab pressings had been changed to a more modern rounded nose, the colour split became horizontal. All

these trucks were intended to be sat on and ridden or pulled along with a wire attached at the radiator cap.

In the late 1930s, Buddy L began issuing smaller models, including a clockwork Greyhound bus, at 40cm (16⅓in). With the outbreak of hostilities, Buddy L had to change to a material that was not required for the war effort and used wood to good effect. The 1943 catalogue listed four large vehicles – a semi-trailer moving van, a Shell oil truck, a timber truck and a hook-and-ladder truck – as well as half a dozen small ones.

Kingsbury's progress during this period is something of a success story. As the automotive styles developed, so did its skill at producing the curved pressings that enabled it to make large models of the new streamline cars, most famously the Chrysler Airflow. These 35cm (14in) -long beauties had enamelled finishes and were available fitted with a horn or electric headlights, as well as with their patented clockwork motor. They were initially produced in 1934 and 1935, the years when the full-size car was in production, and the toys sold far better and for far longer then the originals. The Airflow is *the* example of a car that did not sell to adults, but that, as a toy made by many manufacturers, sold in thousands to children. Kingsbury's winner of 1936 was a Coupé 'n Trailer, a neatly turned-out Lincoln Zephyr with a teardrop-styled boot line, towing a curtained camper trailer. As an extra, you could buy the trailer fitted with a 'radio', actually a musical box. The following year the car was available with further trailers; one with a tent roof, another with a rowing dinghy. A good model of the Divco step van, a vehicle that was designed for door-to-door deliveries and could be driven while standing up, also appeared. The decade was rounded off with a lovely model of the Sky Roof Sedan, a De Soto with a clear rear roof section that could be slid forward in fine weather.

MARX

Marx made such a variety of attractively priced toys that the firm appeared to be weathering the Depression without difficulty, but this impression stemmed from very clever product design and creation. For example, the 1933/4 Fire Chief car, which was eventually made in four versions, all fitted with sirens, was very similar to a 1933 creation sold by Girard under the Marx name. This in turn is thought to be less than accidentally like a 1931 toy made by Kingsbury. Untangling this 'which came first: the chicken or the egg?' situation is virtually impossible, but it shows that Marx employed every device to keep costs down: using existing designs, employing pre-existing tooling to contain origination costs, and modifying the action or finish of the toy to make it appear different. As a sales aid, the boxes for the toys often had simple but attractive graphics, as did the advertising. There is no doubt about the origin of a later product, however: the Tricky Taxi was originally patented by Heinrich Muller of Nuremberg and presumably sourced by Marx on one of his trips to Germany.

Small simple pressings, such as pointed-tail racers – constructed basically out of one sheet of tinplate, lithographed with all the details of multi-branch exhaust pipes and a racing number, and bent and folded to shape with a radiator cowl fixed on the front and a driver's head in the cockpit – were made in a variety of sizes during the lifetime of the Marx company and are very difficult for the non-expert to date. The lithography did get brighter and the colours deeper as the years passed, and this can give a clue to the era. Sometimes one can say only

below: *A Marx Amos 'n' Andy Fresh Air Taxi Cab (tinplate, 20cm/8in, c1933, USA).*

above: *A Streamlined Saloon Car by Juguetes Y Estuches equipped with a clockwork motor (tinplate, 13cm/5in, c1938, Spain).*

right: *The Märklin Streamlined Tourer came with suspension, steering, clockwork motor and drive train, with electric lighting available as an extra (tinplate, 38cm/15in, c1935, Germany).*

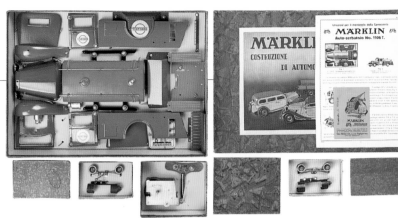

above: *A boxed unassembled example of the Standard Fuel Tanker body, Electric Lighting Set and Clockwork Motor from the famous Märklin series.*

high fidelity for all the world

that a toy is prewar (between 1920 and 1939), because the logo is simply MAR superimposed on X TOYS in a circle, or immediately postwar (between 1939 and 1950), when the circle has an outer band reading 'Made in the United States of America' – unless it was made in Europe! Luckily, if you want to specialize in collecting the range, there are publications that go into copious detail.

below: *A Marx Funny Car with Charlie McCarthy in his Benzine Buggy (tinplate, 19cm/7½in, c1938, USA).*

Marx made trucks by the billion. The distinctive Mack Bulldog was a favourite subject, but its shape was quite complicated to make out of one, or even two, pieces of tinplate. The deep-sided chassis contained the motor, if there was one, and all the rest of the parts – cab, bonnet, back, and wheels – were attached to it. The backs ranged from a simple tipper or a crane towing hook to the much more decorative Coal and Coke tipper, oil tanker, US Mail van and a variety of other vans. The basic shape, despite its anachronistic open cab,

continued to be made at least until the mid-1930s, even when more modern long-bonnet trucks, some sharing the earlier backs, came into the catalogue. Towards the outbreak of war, a new shape (streamlined or blobby, depending on how attractive you find it) was introduced. It has a familiar look, since exactly the same principles of manufacture had been used by Wyandotte: a wheel-spatted shape was bashed out of a flat piece of metal in only a couple of operations. Trucks with separate backs, buses, vans and even cars were all made in the same way.

One of the larger products Marx advertised in 1935 was the 36cm (14½in) G-Man Pursuit Car. A dark blue and bright red coupé, it was driven by a G-Man – a Federal Bureau of Investigation officer – who fired a noisy, sparking gun. This bright idea was patented, and other clever sales ideas proliferated. You could buy a garage or fire station that automatically released the vehicles to career across the floor when the doors were opened. The Brightlight Filling Station had battery-powered light bulbs on top of the pumps. Particularly attractive bus stations, a Busy Street and a Busy Parking Lot were all made from tinplate printed with highly detailed street scenes. Funny Cars (or Crazy Cars) were available with ever-greater variations of action and slogans: 'Is Zat So', 'Don't Bring Lulu', 'Hotsie Totsie'. One of the most famous, Charlie McCarthy, was based on the ventriloquist's dummy operated by Edgar Bergen. Introduced in 1938, it has become a classic piece, partly because of the care with which the toy was designed, partly because its black and white colour gives it a classy look not usually associated with Marx products.

By the late 1930s, cast iron, heavy and lacking plasticity, was becoming a material of the past. While it still suited the shapes of some types of vehicle, it often made the more modern shapes of monocoque road cars and the newest curved-bonnet trucks look lumpy and unattractive. Arcade used it for its buses, for several ranges of tractors – Allis-Chalmers, McCormick-Deering Farmall, Oliver – with a selection of trailers, for fire engines in a variety of sizes and for car carriers (with cars). This type of vehicle was still attractive in cast iron, because it remained 'bitty'-looking and complicated. The more modern shapes worked reasonably well in cast iron for a small 10cm (4in)-long Chevrolet panel van and its ambulance version, but a 1937 Ford Sedan and 'Covered Wagon' caravan trailer, 14 and 16cm (5½ and 6½in) long respectively, failed to inspire, despite their treaded white-rubber tyres and chromed grille/bumper unit.

HUBLEY

By 1936, Hubley had realized that the future lay in a different kind of material, despite its excellent representation of a late 1930s' Yellow Cab 20cm (8in) long, which featured a fold-down luggage rack. And so it began to move towards pressure diecasting in mazac. It used the name Hubley Kiddie Toy to

distinguish the new range from the original one, which it was still making. The first road vehicle, a generic sedan, was only 9cm (3½in long). Cast in one piece, it was fitted with white, solid rubber wheels. From this unprepossessing start they made a couple of attractive, Art Deco futuristic racers – one in a similar size and one bigger – that would have looked just as good in cast iron! But the lovely, single-piece Futuristic Lincoln, with its vertical tail fin, shows just how fast Hubley was learning about the new material and process. The rest of its prewar mazac production of trucks and fire engines was similarly a curious mixture of shapes, with some that could have been made as well in cast iron and others that demonstrated competent diecasting.

above: *This Chein Royal Blue Line Motor Coach was not motorized (tinplate, 46cm/18in, c1932, USA).*

TOOTSIETOY

The market was not lacking examples of what could be done by the expert pressure diecaster, for Tootsietoy was now in full production. According to sales figures it publicized in a trade catalogue, by mid-1933 production was back to the levels of

1930. Tootsietoy had been diecasting vehicles in a lead alloy since 1921, when it made a one-piece limousine, 4.4cm (less than 2in) long, with open-spoked turning wheels, soon to be followed by a group (7.5cm/3in long) of Model T tourers and the like. Six popular vans – all the same basic casting lettered Grocery, Milk, etc. – followed three years later. The 1933 catalogue featured, on its first page, Mack artics, a dairy van, a wrecker and a motorcycle delivery outfit. The next page had Funnies, Andy Gump, Uncle Walt and Smitty and friends in a variety of vehicles. Unusually for diecast toys, the figures bobbed up and down or moved back and forth, but this attempt to compete with Marx failed disastrously, and the toys were withdrawn. They are therefore very scarce, and since the popularity of comic character toys is so great, they fetch very high prices on the collectors' market. The catalogue has a further page and a half of small (6cm/2⅓in) and medium (9cm/3½in) sedans, coupés, roadsters, delivery trucks (including a Mack US Mail), stake trucks, tankers, tractors, racers, military trucks, fire engines and an attractive Overland Bus. Some were available with or without rubber tyres, and most were featured in mixed sets.

right: *This Lincoln is an example of the largest type of model, the child's pedal car (115cm/45in, 1935, USA).*

Though Tootsietoy did not say so, there was something particularly significant about the models (and they were good models) on the first page. An advert in *Playthings* revealed what that was: 'New Hard Metal…500% stronger and 33% lighter than our old metal – This metal is practically unbreakable with even rough usage.' It was mazac (zamac), a zinc-based alloy. Among its alleged 'Seven points of superiority', it was 'The first toy automobile with the new type of slanting radiator, beautifully nickeled', and had white rubber tyres. The vehicle illustrated was a Graham-Paige, as were the Dairy Van and wrecker. Graham was initially reluctant to have its name used, which was odd since

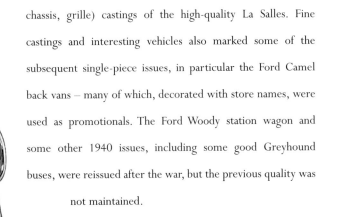

chassis, grille) castings of the high-quality La Salles. Fine castings and interesting vehicles also marked some of the subsequent single-piece issues, in particular the Ford Camel back vans – many of which, decorated with store names, were used as promotionals. The Ford Woody station wagon and some other 1940 issues, including some good Greyhound buses, were reissued after the war, but the previous quality was not maintained.

With its casting skill and the market penetration of these good, durable and realistically painted representations of a wide range of vehicle types, Tootsietoy swept the board. In 1940, its production was sixty per cent higher than in 1933. No other manufacturers attempted to compete on any scale, though some, like Hubley, eventually realized that diecasting in mazac was *the* way to produce high-quality, cheap, mass-produced toy autos.

Tootsietoy had made a promotional the year before and the castings and replication were excellent. A good selection of Grahams, finished in quality colours, was followed by the other three-piece (body,

A few other companies found their own niches. Jack and Maurice Manoil had been making lead soldiers, figures and military vehicles when they broke into diecasting with four large (approximately 11.5cm (4½in)), good-quality two-piece castings of futuristic vehicles: an aerodynamic car with a fin, a

Slush moulding was a technique that was eventually to fall into disuse because of the superior characteristics of pressure diecasting. Its result was called pot-metal because the lead alloy was simply melted in a pot and poured into an open mould, then allowed to cool sufficiently to produce a thick lining; at that point, the surplus was poured off, leaving a rough inner surface. After further cooling, the object was removed from the mould. This method could be employed at home – by melting bits of lead roofing or other broken lead toys – in small workshops, or at fully functioning factories, with accompanying variations in quality. Unless vans, cars, buses, and so on made with this process were identified in some way on the outside, their origin can often only be guessed at, though avid collector/researchers are gradually finding out more information. The Kansas Toy & Novelty Co.-cum-Best Toy production is best documented, because many of their 4–10cm (1½– 4in) toys carry model numbers embossed on the outside, no doubt as an aid to travelling salesmen. In the late 1920s before Christmas, the firm is reputed to have employed fifteen people in two shifts and to have been selling to department stores such as Krees, Kresge and Sears Roebuck.

Lincoln Toys of Nebraska was run by Stevenson, who previously worked for Kansas Toy. In his heyday in the early 1930s, the improved slush moulds had patterned underpans,

coupé, a saloon and a wrecker. These toys were soon followed by a few single-piece items, including a larger aerodynamic tail-finned bus that could almost double for a World War II bomb. The range was small, but the futuristic look appealed very much to the American child who was familiar with the strange shapes of the Buck Rogers and Flash Gordon space vehicles. The production of these toys continued into 1942 and recommenced for a short time after the war. Erie toys were made by the Parker White Metal Co., based in that area so prolific in toy manufacturers – Erie, Pennsylvania, the home of Louis Marx. These nicely detailed, fine single castings, in two sizes – 1936 Lincoln Zephyrs and Packard Roadsters, Ford Pickup trucks and, just before the war, a couple of futuristic vehicles – are now very difficult to find.

above: *A Tippco Fire Brigade Turntable Ladder (tinplate, 59cm/23in, c1938, Germany).*

and he claimed to have made 80,000 toys in a three-month period in 1931. He, too, sold to chain stores, including Woolworth, and eventually employed nearly thirty people, producing 30,000 pieces a day. With quantities as vast as this, you would think such toys should be found everywhere, but the soft metal meant that they distorted easily if dropped or run into a wall. In any case, there was no incentive for people to care for what was the cheap plastic toy of its era. Some of these toys are referred to as 'hobos', because moulds wandered around from company to company. It can be almost impossible to identify them, especially since wheels and tyres were often bought from common sources. Many of the toys are crude, but some are nice castings with quite an appeal, including a charming 10cm (4in)-long Air Drive Coach, a futuristic vehicle with a rear fin and a propeller on the tail. Its maker has only recently been identified as C.A.W. (Charles A. Wood), who manufactured from 1925 to 1940.

One firm, Barclay, managed the transition from slush moulding to diecasting, survived World War II and stayed in business until 1971 — no mean feat. Like Manoil, they made toy soldiers, and, in about 1930, it added road vehicles to its range. It was the largest producer of pot-

metal toys, making more than 150 different items across a range of sizes: army and farm vehicles, ambulances, sedans, coupés, fire vehicles, trucks with loads, racing cars, car transporters with cars, and so on. Many of these were of the same size as pot-metal toys from other manufacturers, and some were a little large, but on the whole are of a superior quality. When Barclay went into diecasting, the casting was quite fine, and some toys were even two-piece. An amusement for collectors is to put a slush-mould toy and its diecast version next to each other on the shelf and to challenge others to see if they can tell which is which without picking them up.

Rubber now seems an odd material to use for toys, but it has all the advantages of modern plastic. Indeed, when Auburn Rubber returned to production after World War I, the material that was soon adopted was vinyl. After tyres

below: *The Tippco Mercedes Benz 770K 'Führerwagen', or Hitler's Car (tinplate, 23cm/9in, c1939, Germany).*

above: *A Tippco Army Ambulance with a composition driver (tinplate, 23cm/9in, c1939, Germany).*

left: *A Lineol Army Ambulance with nurse, wounded soldiers and a Red Cross dog. It also includes a water tank and stretcher racks (tinplate, 28cm/11in, c1939, Germany).*

above: *A typical Tippco Army Troop Transport with soldier figures (tinplate, 30cm/12in, c1937, Germany).*

and stick-on-soles, Auburn came to be used for soldiers and, in 1936, automobiles, producing a most collectable coffin-nose Cord sedan, as well as Fords, Oldsmobiles, Plymouths and a tractor that sold in vast quantities. In all, Auburn produced ninety different rubber vehicles and twenty vinyl ones. In the same field were Sun Rubber, Rainbow Rubber and other small, unknown manufacturers.

GERMAN EXPANSION

Germany's economy revived as Hitler, who had come to power in 1933, put the unemployed to work building the autobahns that were to link the major German cities and industrial areas. Their long, straight stretches were ideal for the large, power-

fully engined, coach-built limousines of the era. This was truly the era of 'big tin' toys – 30, 40, even 50cm (12, 16, 20in) long – and Tipp & Co. made many of them. Tippco had been making a range of quality toys (mail vans, buses and trucks among them), but it really came into its own after its founder, Philip Ullmann, fled the Nazis, arrived in England and set up the firm of Mettoy. Identifiable by its trademark TCO number plates, Tippco created imposing saloons and coupés, both with and without electric lights. They often had opening doors and uniformed drivers, and their elegance was enhanced by the discreet, classy colours applied to the large areas of bodywork and roof. Usually the radiators are generic, but Tippco is famed for two Mercedes: their Hitler Mercedes is small at 23cm (9in) but complete with correct radiator with three-pointed star mascot, rubber tyres, steering and uniformed driver and passengers; the Autobahn-Kurier at 35cm (14in) has a long elegance created by the teardrop styling of the mudguards and the rakish tail, a beautiful model of a streamlined vehicle. Bub, Distler and Günthermann were also making large saloons, but a couple of their toys stand out. Bub created a good model of a 1938 Horch 830BL Convertible, with electric lights and rubber tyres. Not only do the doors open, but the windows go up and down as well. Günthermann's 'Roll-back' roof coupé came in two large sizes – 45 and 38cm (18 and 15in). Its fabric top rolls all the way back to be secured on top of the cabin trunk at the rear. Finished in orange with cream carriage striping, it has the expected technical features of lights, opening doors, and so on.

Gebrüder Märklin had been in business at Göppingen since 1840. Its main production was railway trains and accessories, stations and lamp standards, though it did produce a few grand automobiles. The 1934/5 catalogue shows the latest line, a group of constructional vehicles that may well have owed its inspiration to Meccano in England. The 1101 series shared a 34cm (14in) -long chassis, and there were six bodies: a streamlined coupé, a pullman limousine, an open truck, a racing car, an armoured car, and a fabulous 'Standard' petrol tanker, the last to be introduced and now the scarcest. With a high-quality, richly coloured finish, their attraction is hardly diminished by the chromed screwheads holding them together.

Though it was difficult for many of the other European governments to accept, Germany was gearing up for war by expanding its armed forces and developing modern, purpose-built military vehicles. Other countries may have thought that, along with tanks and artillery, a canvas canopy on a fairly standard, heavy-duty open truck would do as troop transport, but Germany did not. It designed specific vehicles, even though it had to pretend they were for civilian purposes; tracked, armoured fighting vehicles were called 'tractors', for example. Strict specifications were laid down. Armoured fighting vehicles, for instance, were to have at least six wheels with multiple-wheel drive, to be capable of reaching a minimum speed of 65kph (40mph) on good roads, have a crew of five men (commander, driver, two gunners and a radio operator), and so on.

Once pretence was no longer needed, certain toy manufacturers were officially encouraged to produce accurate models of these distinctive vehicles. Lineol, Hausser and Tippco all produced large tinplate vehicles in compatible size. Their products ranged from motorbikes 10cm (4in) long, through 17.5cm (7in) Kübelwagens, staff cars and prime movers to ambulances 30cm (12in) long. Most impressive of all at 85cm (34in) combined, was Hausser's Prime Mover and Field Gun, sold finished in green/brown/sand camouflage and fitted with twelve soldiers dressed in field grey. With great attention to detail, many of the pieces had authentic grey or camouflaged paint, and were sold with military personnel in the correct

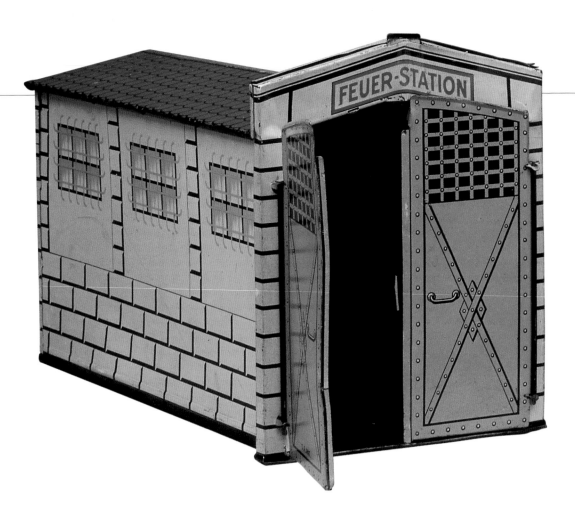

above: *A Distler Fire Engine and its Fire Station with five of its six firemen (tinplate, 28cm/11in, c1928, Germany).*

above: *A Citroën Fire Engine. The firemen have moving arms and legs. It is very rare to find models of this age with their original box (tinplate, 46cm/18in, c1928, France).*

uniforms and ran on treaded rubber tyres. Since the government considered that the availability of non-essential items was a good morale booster, production of German toys carried on well into the war, with some tooling even being moved to toy producers in Occupied France. Dux tooling, for instance, was sent to the JEP factory and was left behind during the retreat, to be reused by JEP after the war.

FRENCH INNOVATION

In France in the mid-1930s, C. R. (Rossignol) was in full production, making anything from cheap, small, cheerfully printed clockwork vehicles, which were the Pennytoys of their day, through a group of racing cars to a series of Peugeot 301/401/601 models. A middle-sized, 38cm (15in) red and yellow racing car was made with neatly folded seams and sported a representation of a Peugeot grille, but the

below: *Wells Ambulances with drivers (tinplate, 20cm/8in, c1933 and 12.5cm/5in, c1929, UK).*

Coupés are more important models of their prototypes. There was even a garage, with an electric light, in which to house them. A 50cm (20in) Transports Routiers van, also a Peugeot, is resplendent in red, yellow, black and cream lithography; it has a short side ladder to enable the driver to reach the roof-rack. The height of JEP's range is represented by superb models of a Renault 40hp and a Talbot Lago 6, which featured, along with electric lights, steering, a well-modelled radiator and a working six-cylinder engine. Production tailed off in the late 1930s into simple pressed-steel models. Neither Rossignol or JEP made much of importance after the war.

JRD was producing a variety of items, from small, cheap composition Peugeots to larger tinplate. Just before the war, these included a painted Renault Nervasport with driver, passenger, and a pig ensconced in the dickey seat! Not to be outdone, CIJ, which concentrated its tinplate production on Renaults, made a Viva Grandsport in 1937 with three figures

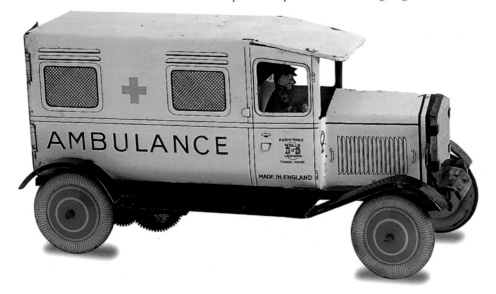

on a bench seat. This was updated after the war with the replacement of one of the passengers by a poodle!

EUROPEAN AND JAPANESE COMPETITION

Ingap was the most active Italian firm, making simple but cleanly printed racers and tourers. The Spanish firms Paya and Rico, which had been in business since 1906 and 1920 respectively, had a vast output of cheap tinplate toys, brightly coloured, simple, thin pressings with sharp edges and corners. Much of their production, from pennytoy size up, was copied from Italian and German toys. Rico's buses, taxis and Silver Bullet record cars in two sizes, 27 and 56cm (11 and 22in), have a flimsy charm. Paya's best era, when it made trucks and fire engines 10 to 13cm (4–5in) long, and saloons and buses up to 35cm (14in) long, was between 1935 and 1940. They also made some high-quality bolt-together cars, which have more than a passing resemblance to Märklin Constructors.

In the 1930s, Japan was a newcomer on the automotive tinplate toy scene. Its manufacturers gained inspiration mainly from America, the closest industrialized country. Japan had not developed much of an indigenous car industry and had been similarly affected by the world Depression, but those who could afford it tended to run American automobiles. Kosuge, Modern Toy (MT), Nomura and several smaller and unknown companies made elegant printed tinplate saloons (Airflows, Lincolns and Cadillacs among them), American outline buses, racing cars, motorcycle combinations, and so on, in sizes ranging from 20 to 40cm (8–16in; a presage of things to come.

English lithographed tinplate could not match the quality of the German product. Wells and Brimtoy, which traded later in the period from the same address, made some attractive vans

above: *A Minic Tourer, a Rolls Royce Sunshine Saloon and a Learner's Car (tinplate, 13cm/5in, c1938, UK).*

– Royal Mail, Carter Paterson – and ambulances 17 and 21cm (7 and 8½in) long. Their buses and trolley bus were emblazoned with a 'Buy British' message, which reinforced the trend already set by the government's imposition in 1932 of a ten per cent duty on imports, other than those from the Empire. Wells-Brimtoy racing cars, fire engines and camouflaged military items have a somewhat cheap and flimsy appearance. On the whole, Mettoy's tin toys were larger, typically 25 to 42cm (10–17in) long, and the range contained some nice, if plain, saloons. Utilizing the Union Jack and the slogan 'Britain delivers the goods', Mettoy's major market was the United States, which was now reopening to imports. Ullmann, Mettoy's founder, had known the value of the US market from his experience of running Tippco in Germany.

TRI-ANG

It was the Tri-ang trademark that dominated English tinplate production in the second half of the 1930s. The heavyweight end of its line was represented by the painted British Racing Green finish of the 40cm (16in) MG Magic Midget record car, and by the similar-length Tourer and Saloon; meanwhile it was making old-fashioned-looking printed tinplate steam-powered trucks. Its major innovation, however, was a series of brightly painted, tinplate, clockwork vehicles – *all to scale with each other* –

below: *A Taylor & Barrett Trolley Bus with a Bus Stop sign by Johillco (cast lead, 13cm/5in, c1938, UK).*

that was christened Minic. These varied in size from the little Ford-Y-type, 9cm (3½in) long, through a London taxi at 10.5cm (4¼in) to the double-decker London Bus at 19cm (7½in). Most of Tri-ang's toys were generic, and its long-bonneted artics with Minic or Carter Paterson ads have a similarity to the American Wolverine range, with its authentic adverts.

Though French manufacturers – Eureka in particular – were producing stylish pedal cars with Renault and Peugeot radiators, as well as an attractive representation of a Citroën Rosalie, Tri-ang's pedal cars are the best documented. Lines Bros' 1937/8 catalogue lists no fewer than thirty pedal cars and lorries, ranging from the Prince, a simple steel pressing for two- to four-year-olds, to the sumptuous Electric Rolls:

above: *A Britains Builders' Lorry*
(cast lead, 15cm/6in, c1938, UK).

A wonderful luxury model with coach-built wooden body. Driven by 12-volt electric motor on rear axle. Accumulators concealed under lift-up bonnet. Gear box with forward, neutral and reverse. Band brake to rear axle. Electric headlamps, side lamps and tail lamp operated by switch on dashboard. Adjustable direction indicator. Wheels fitted 2¼" Dunlop pneumatic tyres with chromium-plated rims and Schrader valves. Spare wheel and tyre. Dummy hood. Adjustable upholstered seat. Motor switch operated by foot pedal. For children up to 12 years. 12–15 miles on one charge at an average speed of 5 miles per hour. All fittings chromium plated. Now fitted with electric buzzer horn, also electric Stop and Go. Length 83".

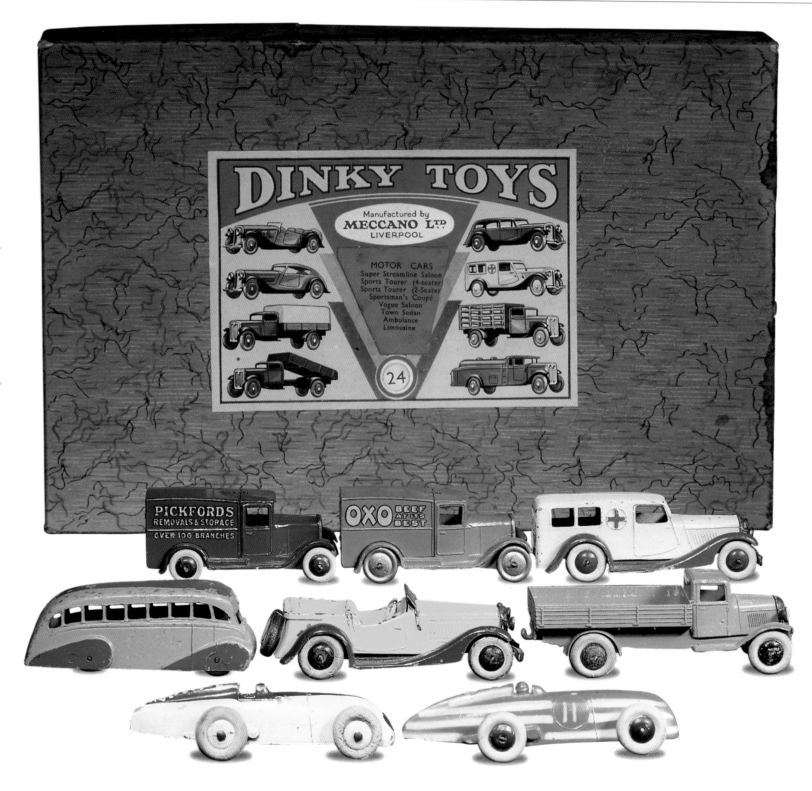

A1008

MECCANO DINKY TOYS No. 28/1

DELIVERY VANS

left: *Four of a boxed set of 1934 Dinky Delivery vans. The plain van and the truck are part of the first automotive diecast toys from Meccano Ltd.*

far left: *Fine examples of early cast Dinky toys with typically bright colours (8cm/3in, 1934–36, UK).*

below: *Examples of the later Dinky Delivery Vans. These models suffer from metal fatigue and can be distorted (mazac, 8cm/3in, 1935–39, UK).*

high fidelity for all the world

By the 1930s, European cast-metal toys were mainly being made in England. Taylor and Barrett, often referred to as T&B, made soldiers, and farm and zoo animals in lead as its main line, but it had been making small cars and trucks for sale in local outlets since the late 1920s. Johillco's product was similar but, out of reach of Tootsietoy's lawyers, it copied some of the latter's vehicles, including its Macks, making a searchlight truck, a mobile anti-aircraft gun, a mail van, and so on. Incidentally, in about 1935 in Denmark, Birk made a range of six Graham-Paiges, with cast-lead bodies and tinplate chassis, that would also seem to be copies of Tootsies. Johillco initiated its own tooling for a small Golden Arrow and larger Silver Bullet and Bluebird speed-record cars. Britains, the most important manufacturer of high-quality lead soldiers, created the most desirable of all the cast record cars, the 1935 Bluebird and John Cobb's Railton, with bodies that lifted off to reveal the full detail of the chassis and engine layout. The obsession with record cars was truly worldwide. Britains also made large, 21cm (8¼in)-long trucks and vans, all with the same cab, of which the ambulances and the Royal Mail Van are the most attractive.

MECCANO

Frank Hornby, the genius behind Meccano, was always on the lookout for new products. He was not afraid to try the new pressure diecasting techniques already used by Tootsietoy, and in the early 1930s, he began to produce lead accessories to go with Hornby trains. By 1934, the range had acquired the name Dinky Toys and contained a mixed set of vehicles, the 22 Set comprising a sports car and coupé, truck, van, tractor and tank. There was also the 24 Set of mainly generic motor cars; the 25 Set of Commercials; and the 28 Set of Delivery Vans. In

below: *A Distler Saloon Car with opening doors and electric lights (tinplate, 51cm/20in, c1938, Germany).*

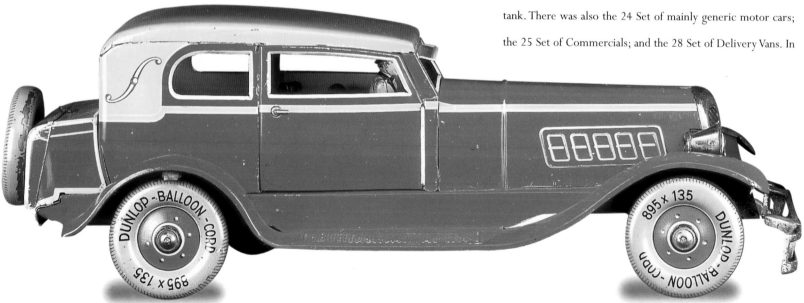

the early to mid-1930s, mazac (zamac) was replacing lead, and the size of the vehicles had increased to what has come to be referred to as '43rd scale'. This apparently strange scale is a result of the origin of Dinky Toys as railway accessories, because 'O' gauge is itself 1/43. They were not slavishly to scale, for the child's imagination has no problem (as the adult's has) playing with toys in a wide range of scales at the same time.

Its house journal, *Meccano Magazine*, promoted all Meccano products (and carried adverts for Tri-ang, which made complementary rather than competing lines), and in a schoolmasterly way it instructed readers how to play with their toys. A 1936 illustration of a road scene is crammed with vehicles: lorries; vans carrying a variety of authentic advertising; cars; petrol tankers; motorbikes and sidecars in AA and RAC livery, and others. The tinplate petrol station has diecast petrol pumps on the forecourt, and the traffic is directed by road signs and controlled by lights. Most of the toys were generic, but real

vehicles were also being portrayed, including one that can hardly ever have been seen on British roads, the Chrysler Airflow. This pretty model, with its well-detailed, separate, nickle-plated grille/lights/bumper unit, is a typical example of the quality of Dinky Toys. From 1935, the toys were brightly painted models of real vehicles, and the series culminated in 1939, with the release of the 39 series of six American cars, which were robust, nicely modelled and realistically coloured.

Luckily the 39 series cars and others were-released after the war: luckily, because much of the prewar mazac was contaminated with lead, a combination that results in a chemical reaction causing the metal to expand and eventually crack and crumble. Many of the toys that survived the rigours of childhood play have succumbed to the silent effects of this so-called metal fatigue. It seems, however, that if a diecast toy has

above: *A part-assembled Meccano No. 2 Car Constructor and its instruction book (30cm/12in, c1936, UK).*

left: *A Wells Shell BP Petrol Tanker (tinplate, 25cm / 10in, c1939, UK) and a Mettoy Army Saloon Staff Car (tinplate, 36cm / 14in, c1941, UK).*

left: *Standard Tri-ang Minic models were re-finished in army colours as war approached. In 1940 all British petrol companies combined their resources for the war effort and pooled their stocks, hence the 'POOL' Tanker. The camouflaged models arrived in 1936, with the POOL tankers the last to appear in 1940 (tinplate, 15cm / 6in, c1940, UK).*

not suffered too much, and if it is kept in an even temperature and not subjected to shocks, it can be held in suspended deterioration. Don't collect early diecasts if you live in an earthquake zone!

So great was the anti-war feeling among the public in Britain that it was not until 1937 that Dinky Toys released the first of its range of modern military vehicles. The packaging in sets is distinctive. While the lid is a plain blue with a wordy description of the contents, the interior features a scene, in shades of green, of rolling English countryside through which the vehicles appear to be driving. The value of a toy is enhanced if it is in its original box, but when the box is plain cardboard or an ugly bubble pack, one might wonder what it is that makes packaging collectable. An internal scene or attractive picture on the lid does make the boxes desirable to some extent in themselves. The collector may find a good box and then work to find the pieces that were originally

below: *A Märklin electric racing-car set with two tracks for the 20v cars (tinplate, 18cm/7 in, c1935, Germany).*

in it. This is an interesting exercise and leads one to pose the question: can such a made-up set be worth as much as a set that has been authenticated as having always been together?

At the same time that English Dinky Toys were given their name, an independent Meccano factory was being set up in France. Its product mirrored English Dinky, but had typically French designs for its versions of the 22, 23, 24 and 25 series. The models were fewer in number and did not develop the accuracy of their counterparts. After France was overrun by Germany in 1940, the French Dinky factory produced work for Märklin.

Apart from it being the nearest country to England, there was an additional reason for Meccano to expand into France, since there was an existing market there for quality diecast toys. Solido had been chosen as the name for a series of road vehicles by an already experienced diecast manufacturer. Its 1933 catalogue advertises *Les Automobiles à Transformation* in the following terms:

What will you do with an automobile in thin tin, fragile lead or papier mâché which will break quickly even if you take great care? You throw it away and you have nothing. What will you do with an unbreakable Solido car? It will be your faithful friend, always to be carried in your hand like Daddy's penknife or Mummy's favourite object. You will play with it everywhere, and if by mischance you lose a piece, you will search for it and not lose it again. You will have become attentive and careful. Mummy and Daddy will reward you by buying you another Solido.

If only toy cars really had the magical effect of making children more careful and parents so generous! What Mummy and Daddy could have bought from Solido were sets. The smallest one contained one made-up automobile, consisting of a chassis/bonnet unit and saloon body entirely chromed, plus six painted bodies. A larger set had three streamlined cars, two being entirely chromed, with three spare bodies. An even larger one consisted of four of these 1/35-scale cars, along with two of the smaller 1/40-scale range. Scale is referred to, in this case, not to suggest that these rakish, stylish pieces are models of real cars, vans and buses, but because they are so much bigger than the nominally 1/43-scale Dinky Toys. Initially the larger ones were fitted with solid chromed wheels, but the smaller ones and all later models had rubber tyres and a clockwork motor.

Germany, too, had diecast toys, for Märklin had also turned its attention to the new process. Their 1939/40 catalogue illustrated a series range of delicately cast models. The small selection of road cars, including two aerodynamic vehicles, was mainly generic, though a long, open, black Mercedes and the Volkswagen prototype People's Car were also manufactured. Märklin's silver racing-car toys, mainly Mercedes and Auto Union, are single-piece accurate castings between 10.5 and 14cm (4 and 5½in) long. One can almost visualize them flashing round the Avus circuit in Berlin. The quality of casting on these was carried over into the company's military series, which resulted in the production of some of the most attractive diecast troop transport vehicles ever made, complete with soldiers as well as motorbikes and artillery pieces.

The US emerged from the war in the best economic shape of all the participants – as the world's richest nation, with the strongest industrial base. Indeed, the speed of the recovery in Europe and Japan depended both on America's available markets and on her monetary aid. However, the most immediate effect of the war's end was on her own industry. Tootsietoy was already back in business in 1945, reissuing modified versions of the Jumbo and Torpedo series of 1936 and 1940. There was a roadster, a coupé, a sedan, a pickup, a bus, a wrecker, and the best of the bunch – the station wagon. Many of these can be distinguished from the earlier groups because the dies had been changed, which made production cheaper by simplifying the castings. The station wagon, for instance, had spats over the wheels, so that the axles went straight through from one side of the body to the other, eliminating the need for axle supports hidden inside the casting.

In general, collectors consider that the older product is more desirable, sometimes because it is a finer casting or a more complex paint scheme, sometimes because it is more difficult to find. A recent price guide put the value of a prewar Tootsietoy Hook and Ladder Truck and a Hose Car at virtually double that of postwar ones. Even though the amounts are not huge, it was still worthwhile for Metal Masters and Accucast to issue white metal copies of some of this group. White metal is considerably heavier than mazac, and Tootsietoys are particularly thin and light, so it is not difficult to tell the difference.

The first new toys Tootsietoy produced after the war, in 1947, were not good. The accuracy of the design and attention to modelling were well below prewar quality. By 1954 they had not improved, and its same-sized Nash Metropolitan Convertible is a contender for one of the worst ever models. Although much of its automotive product was better than this, it did not manage to re-attain, never mind improve on, the standard of mid-1930s toys. If you collect particular marques, you might want an example of its 1954 Buick Century, 1956

right: A Tootsietoy Playtime Set 7500 of eight road vehicles and two planes (mazac, 13–15cm/5–6in, c1950, USA).

left: *Brimtoy Bedford Articulated Boxvans (tinplate/plastic, 15cm/6in, c1951, UK).*

Triumph TR3 or 1960 VW Beetle, but you would probably put them at the back of the display shelf, well behind those of the European manufacturers. The toys are not particularly hard to find because Tootsietoy produced them by the thousand. A group of Tootsies from about 1960, just before the take-over by the Strombecker Corporation, is still a disappointment: six Classic Cars in approximately 1/50 scale; uninspired three-piece castings, they range from a 1906 Cadillac Coupé to a 1929 Ford Model A in dull colours. Despite the competition, the firm is still in existence, using the diecasting facilities of China and the Far East.

HUBLEY

Hubley, which had changed over to diecast toys just before the war, started off by reissuing some of them fitted with black tyres instead of white. The new black rubber no longer left dirty streaks on the floor, was cheaper than white and looked more realistic, so the rubber tyres fitted to postwar toys all over the world were now black. Hubley cars were rather slab-sided and not very inspiring, except for a later product, a 1955/6 Corvette. With a nicely modelled grille-cum-front-bumper, this is Hubley's best car and its biggest at 32cm (13in) in length. Its line of fire engines, stake trucks, tow trucks and log and car transporters with Ford or Dodge-style cabs are also impressive. During the early and mid-1950s, they made an attractive though sombre Ford Bell Telephone Truck, with its sides embossed with a ladder and a Bell Telephone logo. It also has a crane operated by a side handle and a trailer carrying a telegraph pole. Some digging tools were supplied as well. A smaller version has an open back. The same cab was used, with a variety of backs, for other, more mundane toys. Tractors, road rollers and a couple of motorcycles complete the range of Hubley Kiddietoys.

Many of Hubley's products were issued as boxed sets. The 1949 Fire Department Set contained a Hook and Ladder, a Fire Engine, a Buick Fire Chief Car, a cast-iron motor bike and two cast-iron fire axes – the last use of that material. The 1952 Farm Set consisted of a tractor, plough, disc harrow, spreader and farm wagon, and so on. The marketing strategy of selling sets – 'What a lot you get for the money' – continued right up until the last diecast toys were produced in 1978.

In the early 1960s, Hubley introduced a range of Real Toys (Corvette, Thunderbird, etc.) in 1/60 scale, fitted with the latest toy car innovation, plastic windows, and packed in the new style of blister packaging that hung on wire dispenser racks. Hubley was not inexperienced with plastic. In 1950 it had established a moulding factory and had developed a product line of more than 400 items. The late 1960s saw a decline in Hubley's fortunes, and it was bought by Gabriel, which developed larger diecast toys for younger children, including a steerable concept cab advertised as 'The shape of tomorrow'. The move from prototypical toys brought a change in names to Mighty-Mites and Mighty Metal, ranges that appropriately included road-building equipment, road graders, and bulldozers. One toy was to survive Gabriel's demise. The die for a School Bus, among others, was bought by Ertl in the late 1970s or early 1980s.

STRUCTO AND BUDDY L

Two pressed-steel manufacturers from earlier days, Structo and Buddy L, were still in business in the postwar era. Structo had made (among other things) a Machinery Hauler Truck in 1940, whose well-modelled long bonnet had a rounded nose, and the company had lost none of its skill during the war. The 1950s model uses a thinner-gauge tinplate and has a crisply detailed short bonnet, and a square modern-cab style, which was fitted with plastic windows by the end of the decade. The toys were large, typically 50cm (20in) long, and many featured working equipment. There is a Ready-Mix concrete truck with a barrel mixer and a Sanitation Department rubbish truck, whose back operated realistically, though it was not actually 'Hydraulic Power Operated', as the decal claims! This group was jazzed up by being fitted with whitewall tyres. After the death of Structo's long-time owner, its toy patents and designs were taken over – again by Ertl.

Buddy L had not forgotten how to make attractive toys, and it started off well after the war with a model of a Greyhound bus, but buses formed a negligible part of its commercial vehicle production. A bright yellow 32cm (13in) Shell open-tail truck from about 1950 has crude, unaesthetic stream-lining, but some of the vans and artics with decalling on the back can be very attractive. An artic made in the same style is much improved by the bright red Van Freight Carriers decal applied to its yellow rear. This is a Buddy L-invented decal that carries its logo but, as before, real adverts were also used.

These advertising pieces became a standard part of the postwar products, and many are most attractive. One decal, eye-catching in its accuracy of reproduction, is an advert for the American Dairy Association that features a beribboned blonde girl writing a letter: '…and Santa I always drink my Milk'. The advert diverts attention from the oily-looking, dark green cab unit moulded from high-impact plastic. This type of material was dubbed Polysteel and was used in toys in 1952 and again in 1960, when it also made bulldozers. All-steel toys, like streamlined dumpers and more conventional square-cab, so-called Hi-Lift hydraulic dump trucks, were produced alongside these hybrids. Sometimes two similar items would appear in the same Buddy L catalogue, one all-steel and one Polysteel. The 1960 Coca-Cola Delivery Truck at 37cm (15in) long is all-steel; 1961 saw same-sized steel and smaller Polysteel versions. These were reissued with different decals the following year.

As a general rule, a toy with an invented advert on the side fetches more on the collectors' market than an undecorated example, but one with a real ad is worth even more. The bigger and more well-known the brand, the more expensive the toy will be, and if the brand is as big as Coca-Cola (and there

are collectors who specialize in buying anything that is a Coke item), prices can reach amazing heights. This price differential on the same basic casting or pressing has allowed the development of a market in reproduction decals. Sometimes new decals are applied, and the toy is sold as a reproduction, to fill a gap in a collection that exist because the actual toy is rare or too expensive. However, unscrupulous collectors and dealers can pass off such items, even though these may have been made with no fraudulent intent, as originals, or indeed may set out from the start to deceive. The solution is to do your homework, so that you know what you are buying and who you are buying it from, thus reducing the risk of being duped.

In the 1950s, Americans were worried by the belligerence of Russia and the Communist bloc and about the spread of Communism in general. Newsreels showed footage – much of it frighteningly loud artillery barrages – of the Korean War, bringing things military to the attention of children. Army trucks had not previously been a large part of Buddy L's production, but now, with interest stimulated, were featured in the range. A US Army Half-track and Howitzer – the truck being 30cm (12in) long – was issued in 1952. The following year a similar larger piece was released with a whole group being made in 1957/8.

The same era was good for fire engines, always a popular toy. A 1958 catalogue devoted a whole page to a Fire Department Set. The accompanying blurb provides a neat example of the fine state of Buddy L's art:

The moment the young Fire Chief dons his own Plastic Helmet, he takes command of his authentic GMC Scale Model* Set, directing the Aerial Ladder Truck into position. The ladder swings in a complete circle and easily raises and lowers. The Fire Pumper adds to the play with its Electric Air Horn blasting and Water Hose unwinding. The detachable Searchlight can be directed by the young Chief to wherever he chooses, as it turns on a swivel and tilts to any angle. The Electric Flasher Blinker warns oncoming motorists. Complete with 4 Firemen, 1 Traffic Policeman and 4 extension ladders. Electric Units operate on standard batteries – not supplied. Auto-fender steel, Poly Non-Mar tires, 'Brite-plate' grilles and...the Buddy 'L' new exclusive paint finish. *Authorized Scale Model GMC Truck Reproduction – General Motors Corporation.

The kid in the catalogue advert looks ecstatically happy, but his parents were probably just waiting for the batteries to run down.

MARX

Marx was quickly back in business after 1945, initially reissuing prewar products. A new item for 1947 was a sizeable steel bulldozer tractor, 37cm (15in) long, but the line of large steel toys was not pursued. Soon plastic parts were appearing on tinplate items and, as early as 1949, all-plastic toys were being made. Sheriff Sam and his Whoopee Car, the first to use both materials, was a crazy action car, in which only Sam's head and the vehicle's wheels were made of tinplate. Among Marx's new issues were numerous variations on the simple, prewar, oblong body pressing fitted with large rear wheels and a pivoting front axle. Some, such as the Old Jalopy and the Jumpin Jeep, were fitted with tin figures, but the selection of Dipsy Cars (which included Mickey Mouse and Donald Duck versions) had plastic figures with springs for necks, so that the heads bobbed up and down at a touch. An early release was a new tow unit for the range of artics. Still capable of being drawn from a single sheet, the spatted front wings and bonnet were now elongated oblong shapes, though the rear wings were still curved. This is an attractive group, especially if the advertising printed on the trailer is decorative. So speedy was the firm's recovery that, in 1950, Marx was the largest manufacturer of toys in the world, with six American factories and seven that it owned or had an interest in worldwide. Marx even had presence in Japan, where its product – including all-tin versions of the Disney cars – was issued under the name Linemar.

When items were manufactured abroad, on a Swansea industrial park in Wales for instance, the roundel surrounding the Marx trademark carried 'Made in …', in this case 'Made in Gt Britain'. They were usually versions of the items made for the US market, so the subject might be unfamiliar. But what child in the toy-starved days of 1950 would not have been delighted with a 26cm (10½in) model of a battery-powered Pontiac, resplendent in red with a painted white roof and silvered grille, that went forward or back at the touch of a lever? Unfortunately, plastic of this era tends to sag and distort, so the examples with all-plastic bodies and heavy tinplate chassis are not very collectable, though the packaging is an excellent example of box art, with a stylish representation of a black Pontiac on a fiery yellow to orange oval.

By the 1960s, Marx were making many vehicles from plastic. These were mainly non-prototypical chunky toys for little children, a typical example being the battery-powered Big Bruiser wrecker, complete with a pickup truck with a damaged wing and flat tyre, and undamaged replacements. From Japan

came a 'Scootin Tootin' Button Hot Rod: nine levers in the rumble seat operated doors, wipers, antenna, horn, headlights, motor, steering and forward motion. Much of the Marx product was non-automotive and even its racetracks – tinplate figure-of-eight roadways, etc. – carried non-prototypical vehicles. The end of the Marx company was closely linked to the economic and toy-industry crisis caused by the hike in oil prices in the

below: *A Marx Nutty Mads Car, a later example of a Marx Funny Car (tinplate, 23cm/9in, c1960, USA).*

FRICTION
MICKEY MOUSE MOUSEKETEERS
MICKEYS' MOUSEKEMOVERS
MMM
MOVING...
LINE MAR TOYS
MMM
MOVERS
INC

left: *A Linemar Mickey Mouse Mouseketeers Moving Van made by the Japanese component of the Marx company (tinplate, c1960).*

1970s. In 1972, the firm was sold to Quaker Oats, and then, in 1976, to Dunbee Combex, which acquired the Marx name. This group went bankrupt in the grim year of 1980, but watch out for new products; in 1990, American Plastics began making toys from the original moulds.

above: *The unusual L'Auto Pin-Pon Jeep Fire Engine with Tanker Trailer (tinplate, 14cm/5½in, c1950, France)*

Some new casting firms came in after the war. Midgetoy of Rockford, Illinois, began production in 1946, making diecasts in direct competition with Tootsietoy. These were not very good models, being one-piece castings with no undercuts or windows, but they were cheap. Midgetoy trucks and cars, 9cm (3½in) and 14cm (6in) long, sold in five- and ten-cent stores, like Woolworth and JC Penny, and then in discount chains like Walmart, from counter display boxes. The company was into volume production, with 200 different models being made at one time by 100 employees. Since they were made for many years, these robust pieces with tatty paint are easy to find at auto-jumbles and trunk sales in America. In about 1980, new management at Midgetoy put the remaining stocks into storage – these were released to collectors in the 1990s by the original owner. Realistic of Freeport picked up some original Arcade moulds and, using aluminium, a metal available as war surplus, produced Greyhound and Trailways buses in the late 1940s and early 1950s. These were often sold in bus terminals to keep children happy on long journeys. Goodee (Excel Products Co., New Jersey), also produced in the 1950s, but belied its name, for its bad models had no hope of competing.

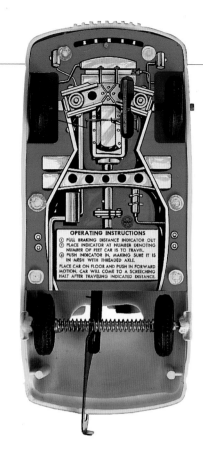

ERTL

The success story of postwar American diecasting is that of Fred Ertl, who, in the words of a company hand-out, 'chose to go it alone in the true American tradition' after he lost his job as a journeyman moulder in 1945. Skillfully spotting a gap in the market, Ertl, who lived in Dubuque, Iowa, in the heart of the farmbelt, realized that no-one was making farm toys. Using their basement and following the principles for making cast-iron toys, he and his family started casting aluminium in sand moulds to make tractors. Initially the toys were sold from the back of his car, but within four years Ertl – who was a stickler for accuracy – obtained a contract from tractor manufacturer John Deere, based in Dubuque. He moved to separate premises and was producing 5,000 toys a day. In the early 1950s, farm implements were added to the range. The quality and

above and below: *The Marx Brake Test Car – a lever beneath the car is pushed to one side by the screw thread on the rear axle so that the car skids to a stop. Instructions for stopping distances are lithographed (moulded plastic, 23cm/9in, c1955, USA).*

the flowering of diecasting and the rise of plastic

accuracy of Ertl's product persuaded other manufacturers – Case International, Ford, Deutz-Allis and Massey Ferguson – to grant licences to make replicas of their farm equipment, for fear of losing out in the publicity stakes. In 1959, Ertl moved to Dyersville, Iowa, where the head offices are still located. It was not until 1962 that it had any need to branch out from farm toys into trucks, and not until the 1970s that it moved into making some items in mazac. Indeed, even in the late 1990s, some aluminium is still employed.

OTHER AMERICAN MANUFACTURERS

Doepke (pronounced Depkee) was another company that decided to go into manufacturing in 1945, not with a new product but with one inspired by the early Buddy L toys. These Model Toys, made from 18-gauge steel, were intended to be faithful reproductions of heavy construction equipment and fire engines. Doepke made about five toys a year, and as new ones were introduced, old ones were dropped, so that they are now very scarce. They were more expensive than those of another newcomer, Nylint. The Korean War made steel difficult to obtain, but it survived.

Among collectors, Doepke is still best known for two early 1950s diecast models, an MG TD and a Jaguar XK120, 40 and 45cm (16 and 18in) long. They were made as dealers' showroom models to promote the popular British sports cars, which were being aggressively exported to the US. They are an early example of models aimed at adults, rather than toys aimed at children. They do come into the scope of this book, however, as they were also available in some toy stores as kits. It seems that more bodies were made than windscreens and other small parts, and that these missing pieces were reproduced in white metal. An all-diecast example is worth more than one with some replacement white metal parts.

Smith-Miller, known as Smitty, only lasted until the mid-1950s, with a change of name to Miller-Ironside towards the end. Its products were expensive diecasts, but it tried to make price a virtue – they 'Cost more because they give more'. There was a small and a larger range, the top of the latter being a Mack Aerial Ladder with a 120cm (4ft) extension that measured 90cm (35in) long and retailed at a hefty $25. There was a similar-length, very accurate, long-bonneted Mack Mobilgas tanker. GMC, Chevrolet and Ford cabs were also used and were fitted with a variety of backs, many of them featuring advertising, such as Heinz and Coca-Cola. When mazac became scarce, the toys were made of aluminium and even wood, but finished so well that they looked diecast. These beautiful, collectable items are now extremely difficult to find, but good reproductions made to individual order may come on the market. The All American Toy Company made large, expensive toy heavy trucks – Heavy Hauler, Timber Toter, and so on – but succumbed to economic pressures in 1955. However, the dies, moulds and parts were purchased, and parts and new limited editions are now available.

Tru-Scale International fared better. Its products, which were made in pressed steel in 1/16 scale, included International trucks and John Deere farm tractors and equipment. Models were made for International to sell alongside the full-size trucks; the models had an IH (International Harvester) decal on the door, and Tru-Scale when they were marketed in toy stores. This tie with International provided a stable market and was partly what enabled the firm to weather the mid-1950s. As International updated its trucks, so the toys were changed to match. Often these vehicles are quite plain, but useful, toys – though some did have advertising on the backs. Interestingly for the size, they eventually had a form of finger-tip steering, in which pressure applied to the cab roof altered the direction of the front wheels. In 1971, Tru-Scale was bought by Ertl, who used parts for its International Loadster series but did not continue the name.

David Nyberg and Bernard C. Klint combined parts of their names to form the distinctive, easily remembered title, Nylint. They started off making heavy-duty, scale earth-moving equipment. While early production was quite small, by 1950 they were introducing 50cm (20in) tractor-dozers, and even larger ones at 75cm (30in). Towards the end of the 1950s, it broke new ground with a toy version of the latest weapon: the guided missile, its carrier and launcher – very ahead of its time, as these toys actually predate the impassé of the Cuban Missile Crisis. Nylint introduced trucks around 1960, many of them being special-purpose vehicles, from a 45cm (18in) Street

Sprinkler to Horse Vans and a Kennel Truck complete with dogs. These sturdy, good-looking toys were a sound basis for a firm that is still in business.

One company that truly exploited the postwar baby boom was Tonka. It made tough, good-looking and relatively low-priced commercials after starting with the almost obligatory earth-moving equipment in 1947. Its early product was based on prototypes: first of all, forward-control vehicles; then, as real designs changed, rounded-mudguard and then squared-mudguard types based on Fords. From 1961 the toys were all generic. The growing numbers in the range over the years reflects Tonka's increasing fortunes. In 1953 it introduced six toys; in 1954 ten; in 1955/6, a bad time for others, there were fifteen. This then dropped back down before accelerating to twenty-two in 1958 and twenty-nine in 1960. Some of the most attractive, though not necessarily the most valuable, are fire engines. A Suburban Pumper complete with ladders and hose reel even had a small metal hydrant from which to draw the water. There was also a Hydraulic Aerial Ladder decalled with the initials T.F.D., with No. 5 on the door. These two, plus a white Rescue Squad forward-control van, were available in a set for the really lucky child.

Walter Reach briefly enjoyed some success in his attempt to be a second Louis Marx. Under the Courtland name, he issued very well lithographed and neatly formed tinplate vehicles with friction motors. There were two artic cabs – the first with drivers printed on the windows, the second with cut-out windows – pulling a variety of trailers, the tanker backs had particularly attractive decorative logos of oil and milk companies. The cars, just over 17cm (7in) long, are single pressings, and though the lithography (complete with drivers) is good, they are very simple and similar to the flood of cheap tinplate toys that have more recently emanated from Hong Kong and China.

ALUMINIUM, MOULDED PLASTIC AND POLYTHENE

There was a short vogue for race cars in aluminium or heavy plastic, motorized in a variety of ways, that could either race along the straight or while tethered to a pole. These are fairly obscure, with Thimbledrome being perhaps the best-known name. Ohlsson and Rice cars came to be noticed when a hoard of engineless ones turned up on the collectors' market. Lack of controllability and variety of action probably account for their poor success at the time, but they are interesting in that they are precursors to the cable-controlled cars from Schuco and Japanese manufacturers, and the later plethora of radio-controlled vehicles.

far right: *A Yonezawa Cadillac Pillarless Sedan with friction motor (tinplate, 45cm/18in, c1960, Japan).*

Since Banthrico started making pot-metal money-boxes in the form of vehicles in the early 1930s, 1/25-scale model cars had always been popular. They were used as promotionals and distributed through banks. After the war, the number of companies producing such products mushroomed as the material was changed to the new plastic. The models were also sold, still as promotional items, through garages, their subjects representing the latest model of each car so that a child could have one just like Dad's. Although these were played with as toys, their primary purpose was as promotional models. While they can not be classed as automotive toys, their interest in the terms of this book lies in that they show just what high accuracy can be obtained cheaply with moulded plastic.

Most toy manufacturers were not keen on following the lead of Banthrico and the other manufacturers using plastic. There were firms that made vague prototypical blobs of cars and trucks in plastic, concentrating on lots of gimmicks for plenty of play value. While Renwal did make a neat line in small plastic kits, for twenty-five years, its main production was trucks with generic logo transfers – for gasoline or coal – sedans, coupés, fire engines, motorcycles and racers that are very difficult to get excited about. The firm was first sold to Chein and then to Revell. Ideal descended in the 1960s to polythene – 'It's big – it's unbreakable – it's polythene' – but it was hardly collectable. It started, also immediately after the war, producing automotive toys in sizes from 10 to 30cm (4–12in). The plastic was shiny, thin, brittle and in pale colours – yellow, blue, and so on. By 1952/3 it was making sets with a tool chest for Fix-It cars, a Talking Police Car and other novelties. Its collectable period dates from the early 1960s, when it produced – described as 'It's terrific, it's MOTORIFIC' – battery-powered cars:

Accurate to the last detail. Each body, only 4½ inches long, will satisfy even the most discerning collector.

With a common base which has built-in drive gear, metal-plated parts, and 5-position torsion-bar

steering...Wheels sport white sidewall rubber tires and de luxe aluminum wheel covers. The plastic bodies

have detailed chrome-color trim, clear windows and headlights.

The collector referred to was a child, or no more than a young teenager, but the roll-call of Ideal's now-classic cars presages those found in many of the ranges made for the adult collector from the 1980s onwards: Sting Ray, Continental, Mercury, T-bird, Rolls-Royce, Imperial, Cadillac, Impala, and Jaguar XK-E.

Irwin used polythene as well, though its varied range did have some diecast toys, including a fairly respectable Jaguar XK120 in about 1/32 scale. But the less said about a Barbie Hot Rod, made for Mattel in the early 1960s, the better. The toys were often inaccurately modelled and produced in garish colour schemes. Mattel itself was experimenting with a Guide-Whip Racer 35cm (14in) long:

Looks and sounds just like the racers that roar round the track at Indianapolis. When the wheels turn, you

hear the roar of the V-rroom unit. The faster it goes, the louder the noise. Use guide and whip-cord to spin car

in circle, steer it in and out. Rev up racer...friction motor speeds it along. High-impact plastic.

the flowering of diecasting and the rise of plastic

above: *A top-of-the-range Crown Imperial four-door Hardtop Chrysler made by the Asahi Toy Co (tinplate, 39cm/16in, c1962, Japan).*

left: *A Nomura Cadillac Convertible – it is battery operated and has lithographed seats (tinplate, 34cm/13½in, c1953, Japan).*

above: *A battery-operated Nomura Cadillac Hardtop that included electric lights (tinplate, 34cm/13½in, c1953, Japan).*

Difficult to find but made in millions by F&F (Fiedler and Fiedler) are cereal premiums, at 7.5cm (3in) big for the type, which were enclosed in packets of Corn Flakes, Rice Krispies, etc. With cut-out windows and separate wheels, they are mainly recognizable models of Fords, with some Mercurys in the late 1960s. These were in production from 1945 to 1987, and during the 1954–67 period the cars were marked with the F&F trademark.

Meanwhile, for the child who thought pedal cars passé, there were car dashboard toys, such as the battery-operated one made by Playmobile, 'The world's most exciting and beautiful toy'. The checklist of working features reads: 'Wipers work, turn-signals light up, key starts, motor horn blows…', then, almost as an afterthought, 'steering wheel turns'. In the first half of the 1950s, BMC was making a small range of pedal cars. The tractors, which could be fitted with a trailer behind or a digger bucket in front, seem in its adverts to be giving their riders particular fun. For classy pedal power, you would want to own one of the products of Murray Manufacturing Company of Ohio. In 1948, it made a Pontiac Station Wagon, followed by a Buick Torpedo Sedan with

above: The Atom Jet Futuristic Car by Yonezawa comes in seven sections (tinplate, 69cm/27in, 1950s, Japan).

fabulous amounts of chrome decoration (grille, headlights, steering wheel, bonnet, side portholes, bumpers, and so on), and then a Suburban, a Tractor, a Comet, a T-bird and eventually a Camaro.

JAPANESE OUTPUT

There were some good imported toy cars on the American market in the 1950s and 1960s, and, although a few came from Europe, the vast majority hailed from an entirely new source — Japan. From the end of the war until 1952, Japan was occupied by the Allies, mainly the American Armed Forces. At first, there was a great fear that Japan would re-arm if it could, so its industry was not encouraged; but after 1948 it was allowed to grow

vehicles modelled.

and goods were permitted into America on favourable terms. Japan poured its economic effort into civilian industry, reinvesting its export profits in factories and production technology to great effect. The subcontractor system – with small parts of an item being farmed out to specialist workshops – was well developed, so that soon there were an amazing 300 or so companies involved in toy manufacture, many of them were sited around Tokyo, with some in Osaka. They were mainly making tinplate toys, often friction or battery-powered, and by 1960 half were being exported to the US. Decisions about product were at first influenced to a great extent both by the American cars that could be seen on Japan's roads and by the American market. The history of the individual firms is obscure, and the toys are not at all easy to come by now, so the best way of describing Japanese production is by the type of

Cadillac had triumphed in its battle with Packard for top place in the American luxury car market, and its big, brute look was heightened by the yards of chrome, the predatory look of its 'eggbox' grille, and the aggressive uplift of its bulbous tailfins. By the time the Japanese toy industry was ready to model it, the rear line was emphasized by vertical, simulated air vents. Marusan captured the look wonderfully in 1951 with its 27cm (11in) model, including every possible piece of chrome on it. The car came in all one colour – black, grey or white – or with a contrasting roof (say, cream with dark green). Marusan modelled the convertible as well, with seat pattern and dashboard details neatly printed on the tinplate. These were usually friction-powered, but some had batteries and electric lights. Japanese toy vehicles are commonly fitted with clear plastic windows and whitewall tyres. The box lids illustrating the contents are works of art in themselves.

The collectable Doepke Jaguar XK 120 Sports was intended as a sales aid (diecast, 46cm/18in, c1950, USA).

The firm of Alps modelled the 1952 Caddy, piercing the chrome of the deep 'eggbox' grille, over-emphasizing the overriders, which had developed into bullet-shaped bumper/grille 'bombs', and picking out the V and crest on the front of the bonnet in gold. Nomura's version, bigger at 34cm (13in), was not quite so splendid, its chrome less extensive and less well-modelled. It came battery-powered. Some of the Convertibles were fitted with a tinplate driver and a passenger. Interestingly, one of the Cadillac Sedans modelled by Marusan was later made by both Gama in Germany and Joustra in France from the same dies. The distinctive Cadillac style from 1959 has been referred to as the 'Batmobile' because of the high thin tailfins that protrude sharply from the trunk and incorporate the rear lights. Bandai made both the open and closed cars 27cm (11in) long, following them with the squarer, more restrained 1960 models – all of them friction-powered. Yonezawa exaggerated the angularity and even added contrasting-colour trim panels on a

45cm (18in) four-door hardtop. Bandai made subsequent models in sizes ranging from 32 to 45cm (13–18in), but other manufacturers made slightly smaller or even larger ones, up to the 55cm (22in) of a 1965 Caddy from Ichiko. ATC Asahi also modelled the 1965 car and Ichiko made the biggest of the lot, the 1967 at 70cm (28in).

This roll-call of Cadillacs does not mean that other makes were ignored. Each manufacturer, including ones that have not been mentioned and some that are unidentified, tried its hand at other American cars. Marusan made a good small 1953 Buick, the style with four portholes along the bonnet sides, and a lovely 1954 Chevrolet Bel-Air, with its winged-bullet bonnet mascot, in grey or dusky pink with a black top. Alps modelled the 1953 Packard with its wide-mouthed grille. A large selection of Chevrolets was made, including the Corvette of 1958 with its scalloped sides beautifully captured by Yonezawa.

Other makes include the extraordinary Ford Edsel – a full-size design disaster – which was excellently modelled in both convertible and station-wagon form at just over 25cm (10in) long by Haji. Nomura and Yonezawa also made the Station

Wagon and the Saloon was released by Nomura and ATC. The 1962 Ford Thunderbird was made, in sizes ranging from 20 to 30cm (8 to 12in), by Bandai, Yonezawa and ATC, while another was sourced by the distributor Cragstan.

Buses and commercials did not figure largely in Japanese output, but fine examples exist, from cheerfully printed tractors – Masudaya producing one as a set with reaper, rake and trailer – to a beautiful Greyhound Scenicruiser and a selection of vans and trucks with excellently lithographed adverts on the sides. A small group of television outside-broadcast vans has cameramen on the roof and the lettering of NBC, CBS, etc. The 1950s were brightened by red and yellow circus trucks, the cages having animals lithographed on the side or tinplate ones visible within. There is one that has a couple of giraffes whose necks and heads stick out of slots in the top and move back and forth as the truck goes along; another has rotating clowns on the roof. Racing cars are represented by Yonezawa's 45cm (18in) Indy car, with red flames licking up the nose and from behind the well-built tinplate driver. Futuristic and dream machines, also a popular product, ranged from the relatively common Ford Gyron, made by Ichida in 1960, through the 1956 Alps Lincoln Futura to outright fantasies epitomized by the Atom Jet. This was made by Yonezawa – 67cm (27in) of green lithographed tin, from its gleaming chrome nose to the tips of its conical rear lights. There are motorbikes aplenty, from staid scooters (early ones having celluloid riders) to a bright-yellow Wegenwacht motorbike and sidecar from an unknown manufacturer.

It should not be assumed from all of this that there was no market for Japanese manufacturers other than the US. Mercedes were popular and neat models were made of the 220, 230 SL and the 300 SL. Likewise, the Jaguar XK range represents Britain, and the Citroën DS19 is in Bandai's Automobiles of the World series. Porsches, Ferraris, Aston Martins, including the James Bond DB5...all the world's quality

below: *The Packard Synchromatic Convertible by Schuco (tinplate/ plastic, 27cm/10.5in, c1959, Germany).*

the flowering of diecasting and the rise of plastic

cars were expertly modelled. Cheaper ones – the Volkswagen Beetle and Saab 93, with their curvaceous outlines – were well represented, although some shapes seem less satisfactory: the short, squarish MGTD and MGTF and the unusual bent back of the Renault 750 do not make such attractive pieces. Surprising and charming in their own way are the bubble cars, the BMW Isetta and Messerschmitt, from Bandai.

Japanese cars were modelled too, especially as the home market picked up and that for tinplate toys in the rest of the world fell off or was taken over, either by cheaper products from Hong Kong or by the rival diecasts. Ichiko made 40 to 45cm (16–18in) -long models, including a Datsun Berlina in 1960, a Nissan Gloria Hardtop in 1970, a Datsun Fair Lady

and, even as late as 1979, a Toyota Celica. Long before this, in 1959, ATC Asahi itself had started making diecasts in about 1/42 scale of Japanese prototypes; it called the range Model Pet. Taiseiya joined in two years later with the

below: A battery-operated Jaguar XK 120 Coupé by Distler (tinplate, 21cm / 8.5in, c1955, Germany).

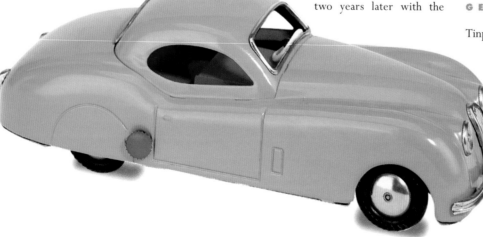

Micro Pet series, with a friction motor, and that was followed by the unmotorized Cherryca Phenix. These dies were taken over in 1966 by Yonezawa, and the models became part of the well-known Diapet brand.

GERMAN MANUFACTURERS

Tinplate production resumed in Europe in 1946 and, to get things going quickly, prewar tools were dusted off and put to use. Lehmann had created a line of small, simple tinplate toys in the new 1/43 scale in the mid-1930s, just the sort of thing that could be made quickly and easily. A small group, including a saloon, tourer, truck and racer, was named Gnom (from gnome, or dwarf). They were 11cm (4in) long and were

given a painted rather than a lithographed finish. The Gnom did not last long after they were re-released because the factory, which was in East Germany, was confiscated. When Lehmann re-established itself in the West in 1951, its production was of entirely new lines.

Schuco, a brand name created from that of the company Schreyer & Co., had been making toys since 1912, eventually developing its famous clockwork pecking bird. Schuco's skill at inventing cunning devices led it, in 1934, to make an approximately 15cm (6in) one-piece toy car, with a fifth wheel maintained transversally underneath that prevented it from falling off the table – a much-copied device. The Examico 4001 (most Schuco cars have names that end in 'co' or 'to' and are given long numbers) was similar to a BMW 327 and had a clockwork

motor and a mechanism giving four speeds, plus reverse and neutral, as well as steering. Unfortunately, Schuco clockwork motors are not as strong as the bodies or the rest of the mechanical parts, and many are broken. A non-working mechanism reduces the value of a toy, but, if it would only go forwards anyway, the reduction will be only so much. The more complex the manoeuvres the toy is capable of, the more a broken mechanism will reduce its value. There are some more robust Schuco vehicles, and those of the type that stop and start as you blow through roof vents often still operate, but they are perhaps the most common anyway, so of relatively less value. Most of this group was in production for a short time before the war and for several years afterwards, even up to the

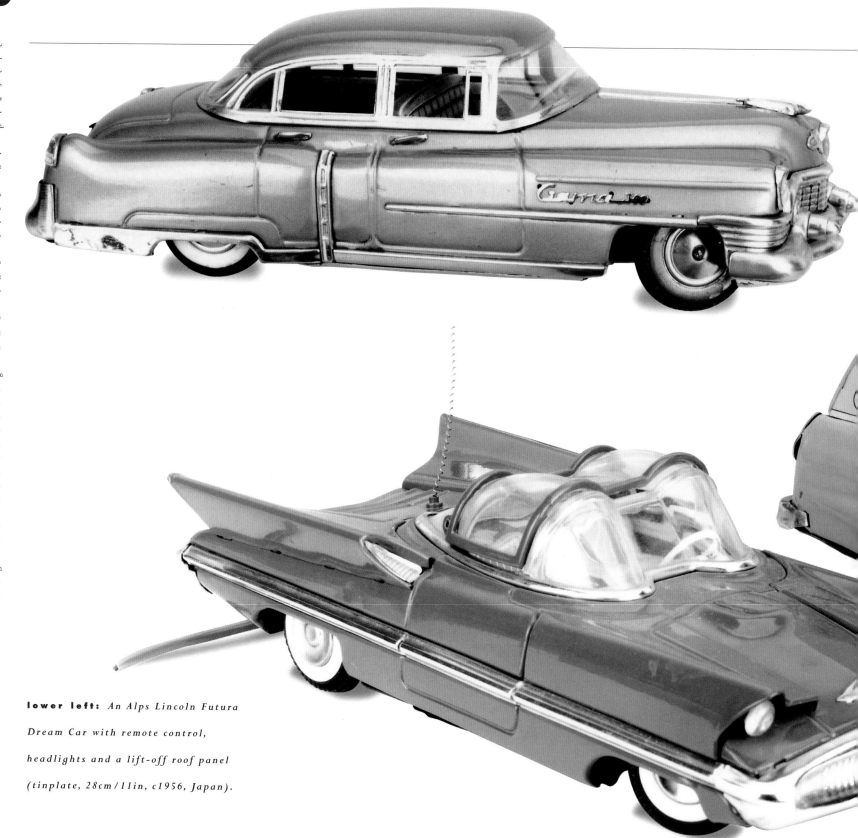

lower left: *An Alps Lincoln Futura Dream Car with remote control, headlights and a lift-off roof panel (tinplate, 28cm/11in, c1956, Japan).*

far left: *Gama Cadillac, no. 300,*

with a friction motor (tinplate,

30cm/12in, c1956, Germany).

below: *A Bandai Ford Flower*

Delivery Van, no. 433, with a

friction motor (tinplate, 30cm/12in,

c1955, Japan).

above: *This type of van was made for promotion or as a toy (plastic, 26cm/10in, c1960, USA).*

late 1950s. This makes the prewar versions much more valuable than the reissues, so it is good to know how to tell the difference. As a rule of thumb, prewar German toys are marked 'Made in Germany DRGM'; postwar ones are lettered 'Made in US Zone, Germany'; and later ones, after the Allied sectors were dispensed with, 'Made in Western Germany'. The price differential between the extremely expensive early Schuco Radio 5000, for example, resplendent in maroon and cream or two-tone blue (and whose musical box plays a now politically incorrect Nazi jingle) and the reissue is such that it is vital to be able to tell them apart.

The Auto 3000 – which had what in German was called *Fernlenk*; in French *Avec guidage à distance*; in English *Telesteering* – was released by Schuco in 1936 and was the first taste of a successful marketing operation. The small, clockwork tinplate

car with a guide wire terminating in a steering wheel located in the centre of the roof, and a set of bollards around which to steer the toys. 'No more sliding about on one's knees when playing with this car,' the leaflet announced. In 1950, it returned to the market, to be followed the next year by developments of the type. The simpler Ingenico (engineer) consisted of a much larger-scale American-style car, guided in the same way by a wire terminating on a peg in a hole in the roof, packed in kit form within a box, with accessories such as road signs. The motor, clockwork or electric – the latter either powered by large batteries attached to your waist or connected to the mains – had to be purchased separately. Later these types were updated with cars that were more prototypical, the Auto 3000 having a VW1200 body and the Ingenico one based on the Opel Olympia. The clockwork Varianto and its battery-powered version Elektro started off with more prototypical vehicles: an Austin Healey, a Buick, a Shell and a BV Aral tanker. These were complete in their display boxes and had an option that enabled them to run along guide wires laid on the ground. Road junctions, buildings and other parts could be utilized to make complex systems. An absolutely complete boxed set is difficult to find and therefore expensive, though many collectors are put off by the holes needed for the teleguide wire. They are most collected in their home country, Germany, and in their major export market, the US, which illustrates the relatively common phenomenon that toys are worth more on the collectors' market in their country of origin. When Schuco failed in the late 1970s, many of its dies were bought by other toy manufacturers. Models, both tinplate and diecast, have been re-released under the Schuco name and in packaging similar to the original. The distinguishing features of the early ones are rubber tyres and a 'quality' look to the paint, while the new ones have plastic tyres and a brighter, harder look to the finish.

Distler returned to manufacturing soon after the war and produced clockwork-powered models and the battery-operated Electromatic 7500. In case the instructions should be lost, diagrams showing how to replace the batteries are conveniently printed on the tinplate base. These painted models, 21 to 6cm (8½–10½in), of Jaguar XK120s, Mercedes and Porsches are highly collectable. That the latter is the most desirable is a

reflection of the popularity of the full-size car and the accuracy of the model. Tippco was still using TCO on its number plates and was making a variety of toys, some with electric lights, ranging from imposing Mercedes saloons such as the mid-1950s 220S to American-style Dream Cars and workaday Volkswagen Minibuses. The quality of the modelling and finish, including that of the chrome, is excellent. JNF, another German manufacturer, made toys of the vehicles that could be seen on German roads, which were of a lower but still reasonably attractive quality. It also produced generic cars. In the 1950s, Arnold extended its production into road vehicles. The Jeep, neatly modelled as a Military Police vehicle complete with composition figures, somewhat outshines a Marx look-alike Hot Rod Tin Lizzy covered with graffiti. Arnold's American-style tourers and saloons have some charm but fail to capture the look in quite the way that many of the Japanese models did.

below: Tri-ang Minic Toys: a Jeep and an Aveling Barford Road Roller (tinplate, 18–16cm / 7–6in, c1957, UK).

Gama is the trademark of a firm established by Georg Adam Mangold before World War II, when its product was not of great significance. In the 1950s, its tinplate was somewhat derivative of Japanese manufacture, but it did make models of German cars (Mercedes, Taunus, Opel) 20 to 25cm (8–10in) long, powered by clockwork and wire-guided. Though the remote control plugs in at a discreetly low point on the rear, so that the shape of the toy is not disfigured by it, Gama had a tendency to display its trademark aggressively on the vehicle, an action that was to somewhat lessen its appearance. It also made slightly squashed-looking smaller tin-plate pieces.

However, it was a German firm that represented the swan-song of European tinplate toys. Kellermann used the letters CKO as its trademark, and collectors tend to refer to the company's prewar production as Kellermann and postwar as CKO, because of the prominence of the mark. In the early 1970s, CKO retooled and brought on to the market a series of friction-drive tinplate cars, trucks and buses of exceptional quality, the deep drawing of the Mercedes cab used on a truck and a fire engine being particularly impressive. The 19.5cm (8in) -long Deutsche Bundesbahn bus, in maroon with a silver roof, is fairly popular with bus collectors, as are the Volkswagen Beetle,

below: *The 'Games Van' advertising many of Chad Valley's other products (tinplate, 25cm / 10in, c1947, UK).*

Ambulance, and so on with VW enthusiasts. CKO's car group – Mercedes saloons and racing cars, Ford Capri, Fiat 128 – fail to excite, and the range is not yet very collectable. However, in the 1990s a Chinese manufacturer considered that these were still good toys and reissued the bus.

Most of these German tinplate manufacturers and some others made two or three motorbikes, many of which were equipped with interesting actions. Some were issued both before and after the war and then updated with, say, telescopic forks. Arnold modernized its large 20cm (8in) flat-twin Zündapp, and the 1950s bike has a bare-headed civilian rider grimacing in the wind. The MAC 700's rider dismounts, swinging his leg over the saddle when the bike stops and remounting when it starts. Tippco also updated its prewar solo and combination machines, one type having the passenger move from side to side as the bike corners. CKO had versions with a similar action, but Neidermier wins the novelty prize with a rider who does handstands on the handlebars. Technofix also made scooters. Schuco's best-known, the Curvo 1000, describes seven different steering patterns. A 1960s issue was updated with a modern-style helmet instead of the previous pudding-basin type, and the rider of the Mirako Peter of 1960 has a shock of blond hair! Motorcycle toy collecting is rather specialist, as it is difficult to find these fascinating toys. In order not to be led astray concerning the age of a motorcycle toy, it helps if you know something about the developments of the full-size machine.

FRENCH MODELS

In France, CIJ and JRD, two manufacturers often referred to in the same breath because of the sometime similarity of their products, made models in a material that can be thought of as heavy tinplate or light pressed steel. From 1948 until probably the mid-1960s, CIJ made versions of French cars, generally Renaults, although the odd Panhard made its appearance. The deep, smooth pressings capture the compound curves of the era well, and it is to this range that you should look if you want to collect the best tinplate models of the Renault 750. Sizes increase in scale from here, from about 12cm (5in) up to about 30cm (12in) for the Renault Fregate. Some had opening doors, but the main panel detail was often applied by a line in a lighter shade of paint, a surprisingly effective device. These were usually clockwork, but later some were fitted with electric motors. JRD generally modelled commercial vehicles, one of their earliest postwar products being a Jeep Pompiers (fire engine). It made Citroëns, usually the 2CV. A car came first, but 1951 saw the introduction of a 2CV van, a neat and pretty pressing that was painted in clear colours and decorated with advertising for Air France, Secours Routier, and so on. This group is highly collectable, being good models. There are many collectors of Citroën and numerous collectors of vans with advertising – all factors that lead to a great demand for these toys. The same cannot be said of the widely distributed Joustra, which also made battery-powered models of French cars (Renaults, Peugeots) up to about 30cm (12in) long.

right: *Over 30,000 Austin Junior Forty pedal cars, fitted with dummy engines and electric lights, were made in Wales by retired miners (115cm/45in, 1950–71, UK).*

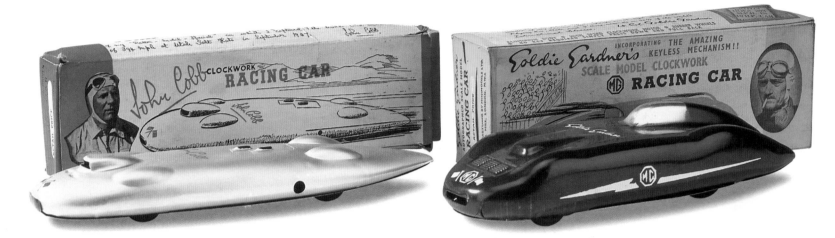

above: *Two Minimodels – John Cobb's Napier Railton Land Speed Record Car and Goldie Gardner's MG Record Car.*

Unfortunately, Joustra also made poor generic clockwork toys, rather like sub-standard Schucos, with mystery actions, including doors that open automatically. One impressive piece, if a little over-large, is the Latil Bank Van money-box with a lockable body inscribed 'Postes – Caisse d'é-pargne' (Post Office savings bank).

ITALIAN VERSIONS

In Italy, Ingap was making tin toys of a wide range but of very variable quality. Some were toys that people would not want to keep; others, particularly early on, were very good models indeed. These included a beautiful chromed Fiat 1400 about 20cm (8in) long, fitted with a music box with a tuneful quality mechanism. Despite having switched over to plastic, however, Ingap could not compete with Japanese production and in 1972 was bought out by Eurotoys. Marchesini had been a prolific producer of pennytoys from as early as 1908, and from 1945 to 1952, under its trademark MLB, it made a variety of good-quality, painted tinplate Fiats, both the 500B and 500C. There was also a 17cm (7in) -long Jeep. Subsequently, there were some slightly larger cars and a bus, but after 1954 the quality and accuracy deteriorated as it reverted to lithographed tinplate.

DENMARK ENTERS THE FIELD

By the 1950s, Denmark had also entered the toy car scene. Before the war, Siegumfeldt had invented the Tekno tinplate models; they were, as their name suggests, partly constructional, and they were nearly all reissued between 1952 and 1955. It is these that one is most likely to see. There is one basic rolling chassis/cab fitted with a variety of back ends: plain truck, breakdown truck, axe truck with removable axes on the side, fire engine with hose reels, ambulance and others. Most are painted in red with a black chassis, as befits rescue vehicles, but the ambulances, 18cm (7in) in length, come in blue and cream as well. There are also rather impressive wooden emergency-vehicle garages in which to house them.

BRITISH MAKES

British tinplate manufacturers also turned their attention from war work back to toys after 1945. Wells-Brimtoy resumed its manufacture of cheap, lithographed tinplate toys, but in 1949 brought out a new product. The mechanical Pocketoys – small, as the name indicates – were in tinplate, but many had cabs in the up-and-coming material, plastic. The early ones have well-modelled, long-bonneted cabs and attractively lithographed backs, and there are some good buses and trolley buses, but the cheaper production has anaemic, flat-fronted cabs with less pleasing rears. There are also a few, such as the Buick, with diecast bodies. Not long after, Welsotoy, an all-plastic, small-scale range of vehicles, included Bedford trucks, buses, Morris Minors, etc. These poor-quality items failed to compete with the cheap and cheerful tin imports that were made by the thousand or the quality large pieces by the Japanese. Chad Valley began by taking over the small Ubilda range that had originated years before with Burnett; it also made a small series of cars, racers, buses and vans, including the famous 25cm (10in) Chad Valley Games Van, which advertised its own products.

Chad Valley was adept at using a variety of materials – wood for baby toys, card for board games, cloth for dolls and teddy bears – so it is no surprise to discover that they made, as early as 1950, a group of approximately 1/43-scale clockwork, diecast road vehicles. These included a double-decker bus, a Commer Avenger coach, Guy vans, Guy Motors and Lyons Ice Cream vans, plus four Rootes Group cars: Humber Super

Snipe and Hawk, Hillman Minx and Sunbeam Talbot. All of this latter group were also available from car showrooms and are eagerly sought by collectors. It is unusual for so large a part of a small range to attract such attention, but they are prototypical, very well modelled and unusual in being clockwork-powered diecasts that were also exported to Europe, North America, South Africa and Australasia.

Minimodels made an early appearance after the war, producing a few Scalex clockwork but keyless tin racing and sports cars in 1948. In the mid-1950s three of this group became Startex, which were wound up by pulling the exhaust pipe! The main claim to fame, however, is two

below: *An Ohta Austin A50 Saloon with a lithographed interior and a friction motor (tinplate, 20cm / 8in, c1959, Japan).*

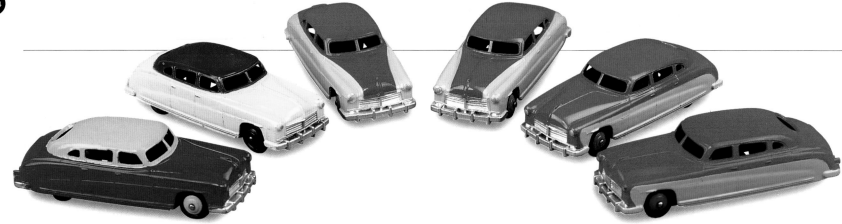

above: Dinky Hudson Commodore Sedans arranged in chronological order from left to right (10cm/4in, 1950-59, UK).

record cars – Goldie Gardner's MG and John Cobb's Railton – both with beautifully pressed one-piece bubble bodies.

In an attempt to get back into business and build up exports, as the government demanded in order to repay the American war loans, Tri-ang scoured the upper regions of its factory for the bits and pieces that had been stored during the war. The first postwar tinplate Minics that it made are thus difficult to distinguish from the earlier product. The more complicated toys – the Rolls, Bentley and Daimler cars – were later released in a simplified form and, by 1947, new liveries, including those of railway companies, were appearing on trucks. From then on, apart from the buses and other odd items, the product became simpler, with flat-fronted trucks appearing, plastic being employed, and the old clockwork mechanisms replaced by push-and-go. The plastic named cars – Riley, Austin, Morris Minor, etc. – are not good models but have survived in such small quantity that there is some enthusiasm for them. Larger sizes were also introduced, including such items as a plastic Sherman tank that puffed out white smoke from the end of the barrel. A large

range of garages in anything from card to wood was still available in the mid-1950s. The bottom end of Tri-ang's stamped-steel products at this time are reminiscent of the streamlined Marx-cum-Wyandotte commercials, but larger trucks and vans were also made, including a 47cm (18½in) van carrying adverts for a variety of Lines Bros products. This sort of size was continued, with circus trucks being the most interesting variants. The mid-1960s saw the introduction of a new range of large diecast cab/chassis units based on the BMC 5 and 7 tonners, the best of which were fitted with a good representation of a horsebox. Among the vast range of amorphous steel trucks was a type with a Thames Trader cab. There was also a new range of Sit-'n'-Ride vehicles, with a steering wheel sticking out of the roof, in steel and a new heavy plastic.

The similarity between the names Scalex, Startex and Scalextric – the last a range of 1/32 slot cars introduced by Lines Bros in 1957 that ran on an electrified track – is not accidental. Three of the Scalex models (Ferrari, Maserati and Austin Healey) became the first electric-motored Scalextric and were still made in the original factory. Subsequent models were plastic, and the scale eventually became 1/24. As the

1961 catalogue says: 'SCALEXTRIC brings the excitement of motor racing to your home. Motor racing in miniature – and all you have to do is assemble the track, plug in the Control unit and connect up the Transformer/Rectifier (or Batteries) and away you go on a skilful, thrilling race.' Slot-car enthusiast clubs were established and still operate. The cars are generally collected by those whose interest is in one particular marque (Vanwall, Jaguar, etc.). No doubt inspired by Victory, which was producing 1/18-scale plastic battery-powered models of British saloons and sports cars, Lines Bros introduced a group of similar 1/20 pieces. It boasted that 'More than just toys, these true scale models are precision built replicas of actual cars taken from official drawings'. They may have been, but Victory's ten or so models are superior and very collectable, despite distortion of the plastic that has caused the roof of, for instance, the Morris Minors to rise to a point in the centre. Rovex, part of the Lines Bros empire, made the approximately 1/86-scale Minix, 'The greatest little cars in the world', in the late 1960s. These are fairly pleasing little self-coloured plastic mouldings of British cars of the period. Minic Motorways also represented the products of the domestic car industry. Designed to fit with the Tri-ang 'OO' railway system, it was in effect a slow slot-car system, as were the later Minic Motor-racing sets.

PEDAL CARS

The pedal car from this postwar era that is seen most often, the J-40, is based on the 1949 Austin A-40. It will comfortably take two small children side by side and was originally manufactured for sale in showrooms. During its twenty-year production, however, many of the nearly 33,000 made found their way on to fairground rides and have since been rescued and refurbished. Lines Bros had been England's major manufacturer of children's pedal cars since the 1920s and was still in full swing in the mid-1950s when its catalogue featured twenty-three variants of pressed-steel types, ranging from the pretty basic to the:

below: *A Shackleton Foden FG Flat Truck with a powerful clockwork motor in the cab driving through a scale propeller shaft and differential (die-cast mazac, 30cm/12in, c1950, UK).*

Tri-ang Centurion, the finest equipped pedal motor in the world. Specification: Length 48½" (123 cms). For ages 4 to 7 years. Welded, heavy gauge pressed steel body with chromed radiator grille and bumpers. Ball-bearing crank drive. Adjustable pedals. 9½" dia. large section cushion tyred wheels with chromed caps. Accessories: dashboard mounted 'Radio' which plays a popular tune; electric headlamps and red tail light with on/off switch; opening boot which houses batteries, etc; safety handbrake; mechanically operated windshield wiper; trafficators; dummy gear shift lever, A.A. badge and rubber aeroplane mascot. It is a beautifully designed car with brilliant chrome and enamel finish.

It is to be hoped that the tune was popular in the US, which was the car's intended market. Not only had this Tri-ang pedal car been styled along American lines, but the language of the description was transatlantic: 'windshield' and 'gear shift lever' being American equivalents of the British 'windscreen' and 'gear lever', for example. The Christmas 1961 catalogue featured a Noddy Car, a rare example of character marketing in pedal cars, and a symptom of the new craze, go-karting. The mid-1960s offerings featured real vehicles once again — MG Midget, Jaguar Mk X — in steel, and even a plastic-bodied Rolls-Royce. High-density polythene was now sturdy enough to create complete vehicles, and soon tractor diggers and other items that were difficult and dear to make from steel became popular.

The late 1940s in Britain was characterized both by firms that picked up the prewar pieces and by a new group: those with technical skills looking for some way to employ them. Among these little firms were Charbens, Benbros and Timpo. Usually, the material and casting were poor in quality and the items small, although Timpo's simple van casting was lifted by its beautiful Smiths Crisps diamond transfer. In the mid-1950s, Crescent made ten fine 1/43-scale racing cars with drivers. Britains carried on where they had left off in 1939, with updated versions of its military and farm equipment. It also developed the Lilliput Series of military and civilian vehicles.

Morestone went on to become Budgie in 1959 and made an interesting range of unusual items – an airport refueller and BOAC baggage-loader truck among them. An oddity of large scale are the diecast Foden trucks from Shackleton that were made from 1948 to 1955.

LESNEY MATCHBOX

The success story of the beginning of the 1950s was that of Lesney. From mixed beginnings with a large-scale Moko Lesney road roller, low loader, bulldozer, etc., via Coronation coaches, Smith and Odell started the Lesney Matchbox 1–75 series in 1953. Small-scale, beautifully cast and well painted, these good representations of vehicles the child could see on the road soon got a grip on the market. The size of the models increased a bit over the years, but the range has never gone past seventy-five. After it reached this number, old models were dropped to make room for new. Such was the enthusiasm for the intricacies of the casting changes, wheel changes and colour variations that Matchbox toys were probably the first individual brand to have its own adult collectors' club set up. When Yesteryears – all-metal models of vintage cars, a traction engine, and a steam roller, beautifully painted and decalled – were started in the mid-1950s, they immediately became a hit with adults. Many were bought to decorate the mantelpiece rather than to be played with. This has led to an amazing survival rate of what was intended as a toy, and though high prices are obtainable at auction for 'rare' pieces, a slightly marked unboxed toy receives no interest. A similar system of replacing models on the same catalogue number has led to a bewildering number of series overlapping in time, and those who collect Yesteryears tend to specialize in the range and have a deep and detailed knowledge of the variations. The Yesteryear numbering system was later simplified.

DINKY

Dinky was back in business in 1945 in time to make toys for Christmas – not that many British children would have received one because of the number that were being sent to the US, where the 39 series of American cars found an eager market. The export effort continued for some time, with the extended use of prewar military dies well after they had been dropped from the home catalogue. There was a considerable hiccup in the early 1950s when mazac became scarce because of its use in equipment for the Korean War, and experiments were made with aluminium and plastic; but by the mid-1950s Dinky was riding high, with an expansion in sales that had led to the opening of a new diecasting facility. There were so many vehicles in the range that the old series numbering system had broken down, and in 1953/4 new numbers were allocated. At about the same time, individual boxes were introduced. This was a time of great significance for the collector. Vehicles that had been in production with the early numbering system (when the models were packed in trade boxes of four or, more commonly, six) were still available and renumbered. This may or may not have coincided with them being given a yellow box with a colour-coded dot on the end. On the collectors' market, a trade box will frequently turn up with part of its contents. It is common for a box to be brought up to its full complement of

below: *A Dinky Export Set No. 6 made for the American distributor H Hudson Dobson (c1947, UK).*

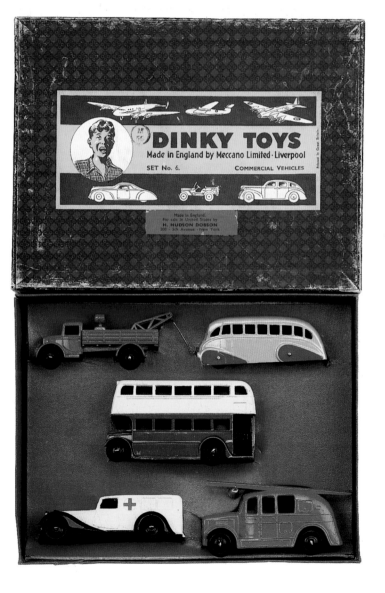

models, but it becomes anomalous if a late, post-individual-box colour is included – if, for example, a Riley saloon in a late colour (say, cream) is put in the trade box. Similarly, an individual piece (say, a blue and white Triumph Herald) might be put in a box with a green colour dot, which should have held the green and white one. The cars in both of these examples would have a reduced value in the eyes of a wary collector. The superb and eagerly collected Dinky commercials generally referred to as Supertoys – trucks, vans and tankers – date from this period. Because of the variety of renumberings and the changes in the boxes during the 1950s and the amount of restoring, refinishing and outright fakery since (especially on models that are screwed together), collecting them can be an expensive minefield.

Dinky were so successful that Meccano, its parent company, somewhat rested on its laurels and did not seek innovation, though it had introduced a neat range of military vehicles. Indeed, it was even slow to react to the competition posed by new companies. Dinky considered Lesney to be no competition – as indeed it was not. It was more than two years after Corgi was launched in 1956, advertised as 'The ones with windows', that most of the Dinky issues were fitted with windows. Solido and Tekno beat it on the introduction of suspension. When Dinky did get round to following suit, it did it well and also made a point of getting the models right by liaising with the manufacturers. The full-colour advert on the back of the May 1959 *Meccano Magazine* announces:

New as to-day! Meccano Limited are proud to mark the launching of the magnificent new Triumph Herald with the simultaneous production of its perfectly-scaled Dinky Toys miniature. This fine, up-to-the-minute new model, based on the maker's own blueprints, faithfully reflects the sophisticated lines of the high-performance two-door saloon. An outstanding feature is its independent suspension – just like the prototype! Fitted with transparent windscreen and windows, it is available in the duo-tone finishes of the actual car. Insist on Dinky Toys...they've got everything.

This car was also finished in a variety of authentic colours to be used as presentation pieces by Triumph. In 1964, Dinky was still producing good, detailed vehicles capturing perfectly the lines of some of its American models, but change was coming. Despite Dinky's success, the whole Meccano group was felled by the expense of retooling Hornby Dublo trains, from three-rail to the new, market-dictated two-rail system – yet another example of Meccano's late reactions.

CORGI

Corgi and its little Welsh dog mascot was created by Mettoy, whose factory was in Wales next to that of Marx UK, in order to chase and worry Dinky. From 1948 to 1951, in addition to continuing with some tinplate, Mettoy had been making generic cast toys, some dubbed Castoys – a saloon, a bus and a

Morris 8Z van in about 1/35 scale. The Morris 8Z vans are quite collectable, especially when decorated in BOAC, Post Office Telephone, Royal Mail or other genuine livery. Its 1/20-scale diecast Vanwall made for Marks & Spencer is an impressive piece. The Corgi range began with a group of excellent models of the stolid British cars that were on the roads at the time – Austin Cambridge, Morris Cowley, Vauxhall Velox – all deliberately chosen for mass appeal. Great thought was given to the efficiency of the manufacturing operations, and some vehicles were selected because it would be easy to make change the livery and accessories to make a visually different toy; the Riley Pathfinder was made because it would easily transform into an authentic police car. The first vans came in a multitude of versions, and, most importantly of course, they all had windows. Corgi continued the successful formula for many years,

above: Dinky Toys, France made the Ford Thunderbird Convertible and Chevrolet Corvair Sedan (mazac, 10 and 12cm/4 and 4.5in, c1961, France).

introducing circus vehicles in 1960 and making a most unusual Ecurie Ecosse racing-car transporter, among others, to rival Dinky Supertoys. When Corgi introduced the first of its American cars in about 1/48 scale, which had all the flair of the originals – the 1960 Studebaker Gold Hawk, the 1961 Ford Chevrolet and the 1962 Ford Thunderbird, to mention but a few – Dinky must really have started to get worried.

Seeing that diecast toys were such a significant part of the market, Lines Bros thought it had better get in on the act. Its Spot-On range, at exactly 1/42 scale, came out in 1959. It was good quality and had a nice mix of cars and trucks. All rigidly scaled, the eight-wheel and articulated trucks are very impressive, particularly the Shell BP tankers, though many feel that the models lack the flair that would have been imparted by emphasizing slightly the distinctive aspects of each vehicle. The range – short-lived, as Lines Bros abandoned it in favour of continuing the Dinky toys after it rescued them from Meccano – has exhibited a collectors' price phenomenon that can be observed with Minic and some others as well. A surge of pop-

ularity and subsequent increase in price perhaps occurs because a good collection comes on to the market. As supplies dry up, this can be followed by a plateau that lasts for a year or two, or even (as in the case of Minic) a drop, to be followed by another price rise, and so on.

FRENCH PLAYERS

In France, the Dinky factory dusted off its prewar dies and the company reintroduced its by now very outdated product, making a minor concession to modernity by at last fitting rubber-tyred wheels as standard. However, it was soon supplied with new tools made by fine workmen, who brought the delicacy and flair that so typifies French Dinky. The Studebaker trucks, it is true, are a little workaday, but the Fords decorated with delicate transfers – such as SNCF (the state railways) and Calberson – are works of art. The Panhard artics replaced the Fords in 1952 and are few in number but have excellent paint finishes and decals – the yellow Kodak box truck, with its red lettering particularly attractive. For the most part French Dinky concentrated on producing contemporary French vehicles, and the early 1950s saw models of such vehicles as the

Ford Vedette and the highly desirable Citroën Traction Avant. In the later years of the decade, several significant developments took place. A small group of excellently modelled American cars (by then windows and white, treaded tyres were standard) included a Chrysler New Yorker and a Plymouth Belvedere, with a Ford Thunderbird and a Chrysler Saratoga to follow later. A range of probably the best-modelled diecast military vehicles ever made was also released. Finally, in 1959 Dinky's old digit/letter numbering system broke down and was replaced by an all-number one.

Solido, the main French player, reintroduced some of the prewar Junior bolt-together models and at the same time a new series that included models of Studebakers and Fords, and one that was supposed to be of a Tatra. This series continued until 1960, with the quality improving dramatically around 1953. Its 1/40-scale Rolls-Royce Silver Cloud, Peugeot 403, etc. are good models and are fitted with clockwork motors. During the mid-1950s it also made a series in the smaller 1/60 scale. Solido is best known for its 100 series, which was introduced in 1957. These 1/43-scale diecasts are excellent castings with very good detail, and the range was continually improved, with the introduction of opening doors and bonnets, engine detail, suspension, plastic parts, and so on. Where decals were fitted, they were superb. New commercials and military vehicles followed at the beginning of the 1960s, and vintage and classic cars from 1964. The 100 series dies were also used under licence by Dalia in Spain and elsewhere.

Another prewar firm, CIJ, got back into business in about 1950 making (usually French) saloons. These simple castings are most attractive, capturing the lines of the full size well, and have an enthusiastic following. Its commercials are mainly of Renaults. The 1,000kg (0.98 ton) vans have excellent paint finishes and a range of mainly domestic French decals: Boucherie ('butcher'), Teinturerie ('dry cleaner'), etc. The Renault tankers with their later Saviem versions sport authentic liveries: Shell, BP, and so on. The Europarc logo was no doubt adopted to make them appear more European, but it remained very French. In 1963/4, CIJ bought out JRD and reissued some of its Citroën dies as CIJ, but unfortunately not that of the splendid Unic van Hafa Motor Oil, or the multi-wheeled Izoard 6-axle Load Carrier and their variants. In 1966, for reasons that are obscure, CIJ vanished without a ripple. However, not all the dies were lost, and there have been many reissues, in particular of the JRD Citroëns.

Norev launched themselves on to the scene in 1954 with a range of excellent 1/43-scale cars in plastic. The plastic was self-coloured, and duotone effects were produced by moulding the different colours separately: a roof or a side strip in one colour with the main body in another. Though attractive, these models do not seem to have been exported and they are mainly collected in France itself. Quiralu used to be aluminium casters, as the last three letters of its name suggests. In 1957, it went briefly into the 1/43 diecast mazac toy world. It produced good solid models that even included a vast Berliet

Sahara truck. Its Rolls-Royce, for which many different two-tone colour schemes were employed, is particularly attractive, and its Jaguar XK140 drophead coupé is the only known 1/43-scale toy of this car. Some of the dies of this highly collectable range were reused in the 1990s. There is a substantial price differential between the originals and the reissues, and care needs to be taken to distinguish one from the other.

Another short-lived, late 1950s offering from JEP was a group of six saloons, whose good plastic bodies were given extra weight by diecast chassis. PR made only two models, both of them the Tour de France cycling support vehicles. The Ambré Le Chat, with its cat sitting on the roof, and the Waterman Ink Renault vans are the best of the surprisingly small number of Tour de France toys and vie for the prize for the best special-bodied advertising vehicle models.

Rami's name was taken from the initials of a range at the Château de Rochetaillée motor museum in Lyons. The thirty-five or so 1/43-scale models of veteran and vintage cars in the museum were partly intended as souvenirs and have always appealed to adults rather than children. Minialuxe made Old Timers, Tacots, as well as modern cars in plastic. These fair models are not really collected outside France and hardly at all in Britain, where there is a considerable prejudice against light plastic in favour of weighty diecast. Many other small manufacturers that often produced poor-quality items – Clé, Gege, Cofalu – are little known outside France, except for the occasional gem, like the tiny Routieres-labelled beer-barrel truck.

GERMAN PRODUCTS

Märklin, which had some experience with diecast before the war, actually introduced its small postwar range with the release of a plastic version of its MAN Aral articulated tanker. The range is in 1/45 scale, slightly smaller than usual, and indeed the models – Borgward Isabella, Volkswagen Karmann Ghia, and so on – have a delicate air about them. Each consists of a diecast body, tinplate chassis and rubber-tyred wheels, with no interiors or glazing to detract from the beautiful accurate castings with their excellent finishes. Prämeta was a surprise visitor to the scene in 1952. With no toy experience, it cast only four models, plus a Volkswagen promotional, with clockwork, steering and a gearbox with three forward gears and reverse, in 1/32 scale. Both body – with the windows indented, not cut out – and chassis were thick diecastings and very heavy. Finished in chrome or painted, Prämeta's Jaguar XK120, Buick, Mercedes-Benz 300 and Opel Kapitän were available for about five years. If you find one, make sure you obtain the policeman-shaped key with which to wind it up.

The late 1950s saw two German tinplate manufacturers, Schuco and Gama, turn to diecasting. Schuco opted to make some of the smallest diecasts, its Piccolo range being 1/90 scale, like Wiking's plastic toys. These delightful, desirable models are solid castings with fair detail. From 1960, Schuco also produced a 1/43-scale Micro-Racer series. The scale was conventional, but these diecasts had a clockwork motor and their steering was controlled by turning the exhaust pipe. The

Ford Fairlane sedan is especially sought-after by collectors, who also seek the rest of the range despite its slight lack of accuracy of shape and detail. Gama's early diecasts, such as the Volkswagen ADAC from 1959, are simple castings with roughly riveted tin baseplates, made for the home market. Though improvements were constantly being made, Gama's range never reached the major league for quality and detail. Various scales have been employed, and there are many earth-moving and heavy-engineering vehicles – all with the GAMA name prominently placed. Its Mini-Mod range of German cars is pleasant and features 1/43-scale Opels, BMWs, Mercedes-Benzes and VWs, among others. In contrast, there is a series of old-timers in ghastly metallic colours that are so bad that it would be surprising if any child wanted them; unsurprisingly, few collectors do.

Meanwhile, plastic toy cars were being made by two newcomers. Siku was a long-established company, having been in business since the 1920s. It turned to the new plastics and issued its first series of models in 1953. These were in 1/60 scale and within ten years 200 different models had been made. They were well detailed, with a broad spread of subjects, and are particularly well collected in Germany. Indeed, they are difficult to find outside mainland Europe. Aware of the need to increase the play value of its models, Siku also made a comprehensive line of accessories. Feeling that plastic was losing out in the market, it changed its material to diecast in 1963. Wiking made 1/40-scale Volkswagen promotionals in plastic before changing the scale, in 1955, to 1/90. This is the scale of HO railways, HO being the continental equivalent of OO or Dublo, and the early pieces (with no window holes in the bodies) were conceived as railway accessories.

below: *Dinky BMC Minivans, Plymouth Sports Suburban Mall Car and a Corgi Volkswagen Van in 'Vroom & Dreesman' livery.*

above: *The Tekno Ambulance 'Falck', with decal decoration, has no motor (18cm/7in, c1948, Denmark).*

Later, clear plastic windows were fitted. A huge variety of vehicles has been made, and in 1969 even smaller versions in N gauge were added to the catalogue. The range has been extremely successful, and the earlier items in particular are widely collected. HO is an especially popular scale in Germany, where plastic is considered a perfectly acceptable material by collectors. Other producers have joined Wiking in its niche, aiming at both children and adults. To find current production, look in railway shops.

ITALIAN MODELS

Italy's earliest and most collectable diecast range, Mercury, started production immediately after the war in 1945 with generic vehicles, but the company very soon moved on to make more accurate models. There were two parallel series in approximately 1/40 and 1/80 scales. Accuracy of scale was not a high priority, and the sizes moved around a bit in the 1950s; but by the end of this period, Mercury was making models in approximately 1/43. In 1959, it had a rethink and introduced a new series, which reused the catalogue numbers from one onwards. It made some really beautiful models, of which the Cadillac Eldorado and the Studebaker Golden Hawk are both particularly fine and accurate. Just as land-speed-record cars were the popular toy of the 1930s, these exotic American cars were the craze of the 1950s and 1960s. Mercury also produced some excellent commercial vehicles. Its Viberti tankers are a unique and colourful group with attractive decals, including the mythical beast logo of Agip. Its Saurer vansare also a much sought-after part of this wide range of subjects and scales. Mercury had the field to itself until 1960, when Politoys began producing average plastic models in 1/41 scale.

Two other Italian manufacturers, Rio and Dugu, both made veteran and vintage vehicles from the early 1960s. Too small and fragile to be good toys, Rio models (mainly metal with plastic parts) were highly detailed and immediately popular with collectors. They are all still in Rio's production schedule and make an attractive display, but there is virtually no chance of their appreciating in value. Dugu made a different group of models of inferior quality, but these are now out of production and have an enthusiastic following, particularly in Italy. There are other names that the real Italian enthusiast might try to collect, but EGM, Icis, Samtoys, etc. are of little interest beyond their country of origin.

OTHER EUROPEAN MANUFACTURERS

The Danish firm Tekno began diecasting in 1946, making a range of Ford V8 trucks identifiable by the V8 delicately cast on the hubs. It followed these with Buick, Dodge and Triangel police, fire and ambulance vehicles. When cars were added to the range, they too were of very simple construction, the XK120 being merely a flattish cast body with a tin baseplate. Quality and detail steadily improved, until the range became one of the best. Its Volkswagen and Taunus vans, with superb decals, were made in a great variety, many of them as promotional items. It seems to be almost impossible to collect the complete range, as every so often a new version pops up that has not been seen before. The larger commercials are well documented, however, and the range features accurate Carlsberg beer trucks with their distinctive canopied cab roofs. Vilmer made a group of smaller, much more toy-like diecast cars and trucks. These are pretty, with good paint finishes and decals, but they were not made in sufficient quantity for many to have survived.

Holland had contented itself with importing toys until the late 1950s, when Lion Car established itself with a good selection of 1/43-scale road cars. These were mainly of the home-produced DAF, but Lion also made a highly collectable Renault, VW, Opel and DKW, all of which could be seen on Dutch roads. The moulds for most of this group were also used by Lange, which was intertwined with Tekno in Denmark and Jefe in Spain, but all the models are so identified on their bases. Light commercial vehicles came later, and in 1963, in a foretaste of the direction in which Lion was to head, the first of the DAF artics appeared, along with a Eurotrailer carrying the names of the transport firms. Best Box also has to be mentioned, mainly because its 1/70-scale castings seem to be indestructible – except for the two Formula 1 cars, Cooper and Lotus, that they also made for Mini Dinky.

Spanish diecast production was as derivative as its tinplate, though Dalia's use of Solido dies was at least officially sanctioned. Dalia made Tekno vans under licence and probably had a similar agreement for its range of Mercury scooters. It also added a few Spanish Seat models. (Seats were Italian Fiats made under licence.) Anguplas was innovative, making 1/86-scale plastic models of reasonable quality of unusual cars and commercials, but these are now almost impossible to find.

Elsewhere, virtually every country with a diecasting industry made toy cars. Gasquy-Septoy in Belgium made simple Septoys and a small, but highly desirable group of Gasquys: Willys Jeep, Studebaker Champion, Chevrolet Sedan and, most unusual of all, a Tatra. In Czechoslovakia, behind the Iron Curtain, Igra was making plastic mouldings, without cut-out windows, of Tatra and Skoda cars.

To name just a few companies in other countries, Micro Models of Australia made a range of simple but attractive vehicles, including a fire engine and a post van, while Canada had an attempt at diecasts (London Toys) in the 1950s.

chapter 5   *1 9 6 5 - 1 9 8 0*

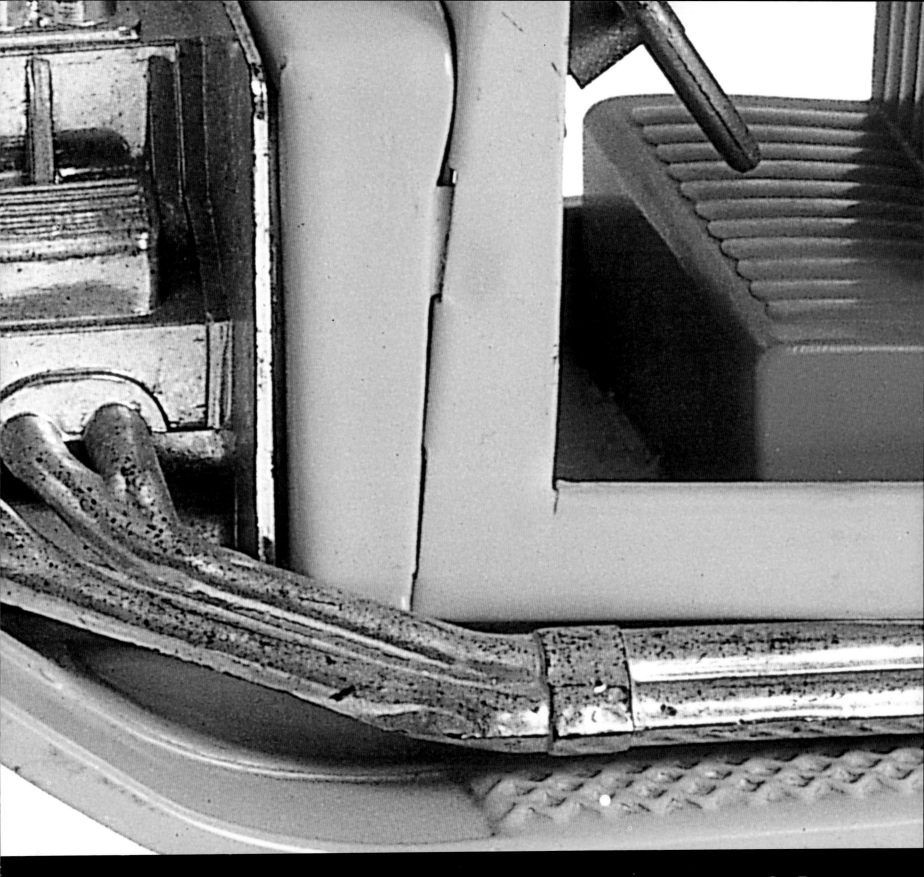

By the second half of the 1960s, aspects of the flower-power era were beginning to percolate down to children in general, affecting the whole population, not just those who were hippies or the children of hippies. The power of the Beatles was abroad in the world, and the passion for popular music on 45rpm discs was beginning to spread down the age groups, making the young throw off childish things at ever-earlier ages and spend their money on music and clothes, leaving behind the 'square' toys of previous years. This was, of course, a very gradual trend, for adults initially resisted the new anarchy of child-driven purchases. It was an especially difficult time for decision makers who were engaged in long-term successful toy businesses: they were used to competing with other similar companies for a share of the toy trade, but not to needing to grab a proportion of the general market. Though some companies, like Meccano, did get into

below: *Barney Rubble's Wreck from the Flintstones cartoon series by Marx (tinplate/plastic, 20cm/8in, c1965, USA).*

extreme difficulties, for most the mid-1960s was a period of gradual change and decline.

BUDDY L

In this period, Buddy L commonly used a very modern-looking cab with a wrap-around screen on many of its 32 to 38cm (13–15in) -long commercials. Styled on the clean-cut, square lines of a cab type used by GMC and Dodge, it is generic but realistic. The interest lies in the back of the trucks: a kennel truck has a clear plastic back, through which can be seen twelve different dogs, each housed in its own compartment; a Coca-Cola truck has crates of bottles; a zoo truck has cages with doors for half-a-dozen different animals; and a milkman truck has rather oversized bottles of milk. The same vehicle was used for some of a wide range of campers produced during the 1960s. There were only a few larger trucks, but one that uses the same basic cab pulling a trailer with three cages is most spectacular. The 65cm (26in) length of the Wild Animal Circus truck – bright red, containing a lion, a tiger and an elephant – is reminiscent of the toys of earlier years. The impressively named Big Brute earth-movers are only 16 to 30cm (6½–12in) long, but, even at that, they did make good-sized sand-pit toys. There was an impressive series of Mack Hydraulic Dumpers for about ten years beginning circa 1965 – if collecting construction machinery is your enthusiasm.

Buddy L also issued an even smaller Big Brute fire pumper, but larger fire engines (especially snorkel pumpers) were

issued in a variety of sizes in the late 1960s. The early 1970s boasted the appearance of an American LaFrance Pumper, 64cm (25½in) long, complete with snorkel boom, cherry-picker basket, hose pipes and extension ladders. With a feature harking back to the 1930s, the nozzle of the snorkel squirted water when a garden hose was attached to it. Soft-drink advertising – Coke, Pepsi and Canada Dry – was found on the backs of Buddy L trucks of varying lengths using a typical concept cab with a very deep windscreen as recently as 1975. More proto-typical was a series of delivery step vans fitted with sliding cab doors and conventionally opening ones at the rear. Most of these, such as the Borden's milk van, carried advertising and many were made in small quantities as promotional items, making them an interesting subject to hunt for at auto-jumbles and trunk fairs. Buddy L made some pre-school playthings that

little kids loved, but among collectors these can at best engender mirth. There was a range of 7cm (3in) or so Brute Buggies in colours from lavender to fuchsia. Larger-size pieces can cause collectors to groan; for instance, the 1970 Japanese-made Ol' Buddy's Rod-ster, 26cm (10½in) of lime-green steel body and chassis with a bright blue plastic hood, complete with silver plastic engine stack.

above: Fred Flintstone's Flivver also made by Marx (tinplate/plastic, 20cm/8in, c1965, USA).

OTHER AMERICAN COMPETITION

Nylint continued to make toys that mirrored the types made by Buddy L, with whom it was in direct competition. One odd item is a highly impressive large pressed-steel van made as a 1980 Olympics outside-broadcast van. Lettered with the Nylint trade name and ABC, it came complete with cameras

above: *A Buddy L Mack Articulated Low Loader with NASA Space Shuttle. The decoration is achieved by stickers (tin/plastic, 28cm/11in, c1979, Japan).*

and cables. By now, large toys such as these were being packed in open-fronted, thick corrugated cardboard boxes that displayed the contents clearly on shop shelves. They held together so well that it was frequently difficult to get the toy out without tearing the box, and it is rare to find complete packaging from this era. The Olympics van may have survived intact simply because souvenirs of the Moscow Olympics did not sell well in those countries that withdrew from the Olympic Games after a row over the Russian invasion of Afghanistan.

By the mid-1970s, Tonka was also thriving, with Tonka Corporation established in Canada, Tonka Limited in the UK and Tonka Gmbh in Germany. Its catalogue, or *Look Book* lists, on the front 'Five ways to look at Tonka Toys', which sum up their marketing strategy:

❶ **Look at the strength. Virtually all Tonka Toys include extra strong axles that won't bend even under the standing weight of a 200-pound adult.**

❷ **Look at the steel. There's a lot of it in Tonka Toys...and it's the same thickness found in the bodies and fenders of new cars.**

❸ **Look at the tyres. They're guaranteed for the life of the toy. And they're attached to stay on, even under severe play conditions.**

❹ **Look at the realism. Realistic proportions. Realistic details. And realistic functions performed by working mechanisms on many models.**

❺ **Look at the finish. Two coats of real truck enamel protect all steel toys. It's highly chip resistant. Non-toxic. Dip-coating and electrostatic spraying provide total coverage to protect metal against rust.**

Persuasive words – indeed, the answer to a parent's prayer! Small Tonka-Tote toys could be purchased with the by-now obligatory launch ramp. Sizes increased, from Funnies, Hot-rods and the like, through a low loader with bulldozer and car transporters in three sizes to impressive action earth-movers, including the Mighty-Tonka crane, 76cm (30in) long, complete with swivelling grab-bucket and realistic action. Based on reality they may have been, but most make no pretence at all to being models rather than toys.

This period saw the brief appearance of a number of firms whose small product ranges fascinate the collector because they are uncommon. Finding a Cigarbox model, packed in a carton similar to that from which the product got its name (obviously derived from that of Matchbox), might well arouse one's interest in this group of 1/60–1/70 toys, made by Aurora in 1969, with plastic bodies and diecast chassis. Their nicely detailed mouldings have the

decoration spray-painted on, a system cheaper than that of applying a decal. The more familiar name of Champ of the Road appeared in the late 1970s. This was an American marketing company whose 1/50-scale trucks, with diecast cabs and plastic backs, were made in Hong Kong by Universal. At the time, the range also included some reasonable diecast cars. Sourcing from Hong Kong was to become an increasing feature of American and, subsequently, European toy production, as companies in the First World were hit by rising labour prices and economic recession. The reputation that Hong Kong had for producing 'rubbish'

below: *A Buddy L 'Ol Buddy's Rod Ster' with a steel body and chassis and plastic seats, hood and engine (steel/plastic, 27cm/10.5in, c1970, Japan).*

above: *A typical example of the Mattel 'Hot Wheels' Hot Rod (5-6cm/2–2.5in, c1975, Hong Kong).*

was soon swept away as the Far East began to develop into a major zone of manufacturing.

Ertl was going from strength to strength in the 1970s. It had already begun to branch out from farm toys and, to broaden its base away from farming areas, had decided to sell to the general retailer. In 1964 it produced its first trade catalogue. A national sales force was established, and in 1967 Ertl became a subsidiary of the Victor Comptometer Corporation. Victor considered the move to sell to traditional toy outlets very important; it provided capital to consolidate Ertl and enable it to buy companies such as Structo. Towards the end of this period, becoming even more successful, Ertl began to branch into the hobby market. In 1977, however, the whole of Victor and its subsidiaries merged with Kidde Inc., a move that saw it become just one of the 180 companies owned by Kidde worldwide and set Ertl up to face the rigours of the times. One of the first steps was to send dies to whichever part of the world would be able to produce the toys most cheaply, beginning with Hong Kong, rather than manufacturing only in Dyersville.

HOT WHEELS

Topper Toys had been one of the manufacturers that had built up its trade using a lot of plastic in its products to satisfy the increasing demand for toys that accompanied the postwar baby-boomer years. It had gone on to develop a popular line under its Johnny Lightning name, consisting of custom-car types based loosely on full-size vehicles. Topper had a Custom Ferrari and XKE, as well as a Custom Spoiler and Turbine, a Frantic Ferrari and a Sand Stormer that would run on a raceway set with track and speed launchers. Unhappily for Topper and many other companies, Mattel launched Hot Wheels in 1968. The idea was not Mattel's, or Topper's, or even Marx's, who sold its Loop-the-Loop racer set in 1931. The latter had a tiny car 4½cm (1¾in) long positioned at the top of a tinplate track that terminated in a run-off from a 360° loop, allowing the car to whiz across the floor. The new idea was the same as that of any child who has ever rolled a stone down a hill, or a spool of thread down a slope, but Mattel picked it up, packaged it, and exploited it for all it was worth.

The first production vehicle, a Chevrolet Camaro, was ready in May 1968. As the catalogue says: 'Hot Wheels are the fastest metal cars in the world! They don't need batteries, or electric current, or motors – yet they out-race, out-stunt, out-distance every other miniature metal car on Hot Wheels Action Sets...'. The cars and the sets were custom-made for each other, but it is an impressive enough claim anyway. 'Hot Wheels are THE custom class cars for collectors.

They're California Custom styled with red stripe tyres, "mag" wheels, moving parts, wild, California paint jobs! Hot Wheels are for the collector who likes to race.' This collector was the boy, not the adult. The secret of Hot Wheel's success lay on the next page: 'Exclusive Torsion-Bar Suspension. Low-Friction Wheel Bearings! Go Faster…roll farther on.'

The thin-axled, low-friction toy was backed up with a host of marketing ploys, such as the collectors' button in each bubble pack. The cars – Cougar, Mustang, T-bird, Barracuda, Corvette, and so on – were bound to be popular, finished in brilliant colours with lots of extras sticking out, just like the real custom cars that any child could now see on television. Several sets of curved and angled tracks were available; the cars raced around by gravity, but almost immediately Super-charger impeller units were available to give added oomph. Collector cases were supplied to house your precious cars.

The sixteen models were initially made in the United States, but by 1972 all were being made in Hong Kong. Each car (the original custom cars being followed by a line of futuristic vehicles) was available in ten or more Spectraflame colours. Every year, changes were made to the products and new lines were added. In 1970 Mattel added an engine to a group and called them Sizzlers. In 1979 there was a character merchandising line, The Heroes, which included Spiderman. To promote its product, Mattel sponsored race teams, and in 1971 Hot Wheels teams could be seen in action in drag races not only in the US but also in Britain at the Santa Pod Raceway. Constant invention and renewal of the appeal of the product paid off handsomely.

above: *The Tootsietoy '63 Chevy Corvette' and '40 Ford' – neither has a motor or steering (diecast metal and plastic, 13cm/5in, c1970, Hong Kong).*

COLLECTORS' ITEMS

In the mid-1960s, the Hess division of the Amerada Hess Corporation, a company completely separate from the prewar German Hess toy company, ran petrol and service stations. In 1964, Hess put an oil-tanker toy on sale in these stations. After the success of the first, it continued to issue a new one annually at about the same time of year, just in time for dad to be badgered into buying one as a Christmas present.

below and right: Two typical cheap lithographed cars from the late 1960s and 1970s. The left model was made in Hong Kong, the right in Japan.

The good-quality plastic models of Hess tankers were made by Marx in Hong Kong until the 1970s. They came complete with batteries, and the boxes were strong and well designed. As an additional incentive to purchase, a savings bank feature was added in the early 1980s. These attractive models were issued for sale as promotional items, but many will have been played with as toys. Most, however, remain perfect in their boxes and, having caught the imagination of the adult, are enjoyable to collect. General rules – such as that the lack of a box or damage to the model reduces the value on the collectors' market – still apply, but this is such a specialist area that few are likely to know which year's issue is scarce (and therefore expensive) or common (and thus cheap). If you want to collect them seriously, as opposed to picking one up because you like it, the best bet is a good price guide.

In the mid-1960s, a new family firm called Winross was established to make toys based on White trucks, and demand for its toys built quickly. The decalling was applied by the silk-screen process, which gives excellent repeatable results at a reasonable cost. The demand for these models as promotionals from companies that ran White trucks was strong, and the word *toys* on the packaging was diminished in size; soon all pretence of their being playthings was dropped. The vehicles are about 1/64 scale and rather simple in shape to allow for the automated silk-screen decalling process. There was also the demand from collectors, and some of each run was diverted to them, via a separate marketing company. In 1976, the 'promotional only' policy was suspended for the production of thirteen Bicentennial commemoratives portraying the original States of the Union. Immensely attractive, these sets were eagerly sought by collectors, many of whom thought that they would appreciate in value. They did not take into account, however, the quantities made or that the sets would be a brief enthusiasm, much like yesterday's newspaper. Winross has its own following, and its story is not unique. It is, however, one of the earliest and best-documented examples of how current toys for children turn into models for collectors.

As the collectors' market built up during the 1970s, so did the demand for replacement parts. Kenton and Arcade cast-iron parts were easily broken or lost, and whole chassis or drivers, for example, were recast in lead. Indeed, entire cast-iron items were re-created in lead or, later, cast iron. In general, a cast-iron piece that is riveted together is probably original, while one that is screwed together is almost certainly not. Tyres were made to fit all sizes and shapes of 1930s toys, one could buy new axles for Tootsietoys. Eccles

of Burlington, Iowa, even had an extensive catalogue of slush pieces recast from the original moulds. Let the collector beware!

JAPANESE PRODUCTS

In the early 1960s, Japan was producing quality diecasts in 1/43 scale, the first ones being simple castings with tinplate bases. These arrived in Europe and America only by means of exchanges between collectors. It was not that they were made for collectors (they weren't), for these models of Japanese cars were intended for sale at home. Indeed, outside their home country, Japanese cars were then an unusual sight on the roads, and they were often spoken of in derogatory tones. How wrong can you be! Japanese car makers began in familiar style by mimicking the West and then surpassing it in quality,

below: *A Zee Toys Turbo Trans Am with a 'pull-back-and-let-go' motor (diecast, 10cm/4in, c1980, Hong Kong).*

reliability and design. The toy manufacturers followed the same pattern. Around 1964, Cherryca Phenix began plating its models before painting them. This not only gave a lustrous paint finish, but enabled the window surrounds to be realistically chromed by leaving them free of paint. The bases were cast, opening parts were fitted, and the bonnet could be lifted to reveal the engine – often fitted with a five- instead of a six-terminal battery. Little mistakes like this may have caused great hilarity abroad, but the laughter subsided when people realized that Model Pet, brand name of Asahi, had invented a method of opening the bonnet of its Toyota Sport 800 that not only gave it a wonderful fit and a realistic action, but also managed to circumvent the many patents that Solido had taken out in an attempt to dominate the market. A few Model Pet cars were fitted with electric lights and other gim-

below: *The detailed and accurate Ford Thunderbird and Capri by Solido (diecast, 10cm/4in, 1965-80, France).*

micks, but the most desirable of the early versions are – as so often – a group of American cars: Dodge, Ford, Chevrolet and Buick. In the 1960s, there were not many collectors of Japanese diecasts, either in Japan or abroad, so the quantity of mint boxed models is very small. The demand, particularly from Japanese collectors, who understandably want their toys back, is high – and so are the prices. As time went on, Asahi product began to decline and there was little comparison between a 1965 Toyota Corona, with its finely chased grille and its last model, a Datsun Cedric of circa 1973, which were not exported in any quantity, and there is little interest in them.

Diapet, a brand name of Yonezawa Toys, one of whose trademarks is its initial letter Y, embarked on an ambitious programme. From 1965 to 1970, its models were 1/43 scale, but by 1980 they had varied widely, from the larger 1/40 to the much larger 1/30, as it was perceived that children liked bigger toy cars. An early gem was the Diapet Porsche 911, along with a Nissan Sylvia Coupé and a Datsun Fairlady Sports with well-fitting opening parts. The bulk of its product was

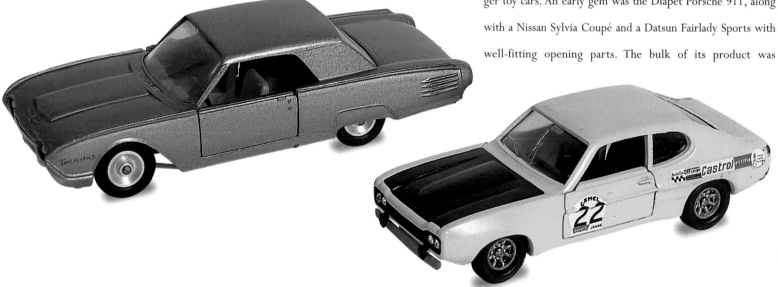

modelled on Japanese prototypes, though the occasional top-of-the-range European or American car was also made. Collecting Diapet is complicated by the fact that most of its catalogues are in Japanese, and by frequent renumberings, in 1972, 1973, 1974 and 1977. Each model was made for only three or four years before being updated. This is another reason for their scarcity, compared with makes like Dinky that kept on producing a toy as long as it kept selling. Around the end of the

1960s, there was a poorly documented marketing tie-up between Yonezawa and the American importer Cragstan that led to a group of Sabra (Israel) American cars being labelled 'Detroits' in a Japanese catalogue. Sablon from Belgium were also in the same catalogue. One American car that must win the prize for the most over-the-top Yonezawa vehicle is its 1980-ish Lincoln Hearse, fitted out with a gilt

above: *The Ichiko Ford Taunus Driving School Car with remote control (tinplate, 23cm/9in, c1965, Japan).*

plastic rear superstructure of pagoda roof with flying dragon. It proved instantly popular among collectors! Sakura was the name coined for the Yonezawa Super Car range, which was briefly available from 1976, the first being a 1/43-scale Lamborghini Miura. Models with better detailing followed in its well-collected World Famous Car Series, including a Rolls-Royce and some American subjects.

From its base of being a general toy-producing company, Tomy started production of the Tomica range in 1971 with six diecast cars in scales from 1/60 to 1/65. Reminiscent of Matchbox 1–75s, they fit a standard box. From the start, their play value was enhanced with plastic garages, multi-storey car parks and the like. Tomy's first year of serious entry into the model-car field saw the production of thirty models, with twelve more listed as 'coming soon'. Tomy started as if it meant to go on, and the range is still in production. A short time after Tomica began, Tomica Dandys were released. The mixed scales, 1/40 to 1/50, of this larger series cause anomalies that annoy the collector, but not the child: its 1/49 Toyota Crown Saloon ends up smaller than the (in full size shorter) Honda Civic, which was modelled in 1/43 scale. In the late 1970s, Edai Grip produced a small range of well-made Formula 1 racing cars and super-cars in 1/43 scale, and a selection in the considerably larger 1/20 to 1/28 scales. Kado, which started around the same time, worked in a variety of scales, making some lovely road cars and, most interestingly, a group of vans with fine decalling.

DINKY CHANGES HANDS

The mid-1960s was the time of the most significant amalgamations of toy-companies in Britain, when the successful Lines Bros group rescued the ailing Meccano Company. The combination should have been a world-beating one, as Lines Bros

below: *The Chevrolet Corvette Stingray by Kidco (diecast, 16cm/6.5in, 1974, Hong Kong).*

brought to it the inventiveness behind Dinky, once the world's most popular 1/43-scale diecasts. Lines was sufficiently impressed with the existing and planned range of Dinky Toys that they put their full energy into it and allowed its own Spot-On Range of vehicles to fade quietly away in the three or so years following 1961. Rumours abounded in the collecting fraternity, whose network now spread throughout the First World, of a fire at the Tri-ang factory in Ireland having destroyed the dies…thus providing an early lesson in not believing all you hear. The prosaic truth that a firm acts for economic reasons in discontinuing a range was considered too uninteresting a story to be credible!

Despite its promise, Dinky rather wallowed in the late 1960s, apparently without much direction. It toyed with character merchandising, a potential gold-mine, their first coup being Gerry Anderson's puppet television series *Thunderbirds*, but who has ever heard of Stripey the Magic Mini with Candy, Andy and the Bearandas? The coloured stripes on the Mini are of such poor quality that even an example that has never been out of its packaging may not be of the quality usually expected in a mint boxed item. Highly sought-after by Mini collectors, who may not care about the figures, the striped versions are

very difficult to find in a condition to satisfy the pernickety collector. In the late 1960s, Dinky introduced speedwheels, as did every other maker, so powerful was the threat of Mattel's Hot Wheels. Building on work already started by Lines Bros, it also made a long-lived range of military models. In an attempt to keep costs down, stickers were substituted for transfer decals, and it made half a dozen models in 1/42 scale for export to America. These Hong Kong Dinks, as they are colloquially known, were of poor quality, and the project was abandoned.

above: *A Rambler Marlin and an Oldsmobile 88, typical late 1960s Corgi models (diecast, 10cm/4in, c1966, UK).*

The year 1971 was a bad one. The whole of the Lines group went into liquidation, when, alarmed by a general recession in the toy trade, the bank called in its heavy loans. Dinky ended up in the hands of Airfix, which had been specializing in the manufacture of plastic kits since just after the war. An attempt to break into the large size with 1/25-scale cars was not a success – surely it could have chosen a better subject than the Ford Capri, popular though it was with young men? Some of the standard models were packaged as metal kits complete with paints. A few large steel Mogul toys were introduced to compete with Tonka. There was an increasing use of plastic parts to keep costs down – but all to no avail. Collectors wrote to Dinky complaining about a choice of subjects that pleased neither the child nor the adult, but the collectors' market was dismissed as unimportant. Amid the economic disarray and strikes of 1979, the factory closed. Matchbox eventually bought the Dinky name in 1987 but none of the dies; in 1988, it released the so-called 'Dinky Collection', a new set of models for adults!

CORGI'S UPS AND DOWNS

By contrast, in 1965 Corgi was riding high, though without relying on TV puppets. It went to the top, securing the rights to James Bond 007's Aston Martin. When it came out, it created such a craze that, in staff canteens, before giving the toy to their son, grown men would be seen 'testing' the mechanism that fired the gunman through the opening roof, covering their teacups to stop the passenger from falling in. The Corgi production list for that year is astounding: January – eight existing castings refinished as military vehicles; February – Ferrari Berlinetta, a Monte Carlo Rally Mini Cooper S, a Farm Tipper; March – Walls Ice Cream Van, Joe's Diner Mobile Canteen (re-colour), Rover 2000 Rally Car, the Saint's Volvo P1800, Mini Countryman with surfer, Forward Control Jeep, a farm and a rally gift set; April – 1910 Renault 12/16, Ford Mustang; and so on. A mere year after Hot Wheels first rolled, Corgi replied

with Rockets, and the next year Whizzwheels were fitted to the main range, giving an unfortunate non-prototypical appearance. Corgi's reaction to the slump in 1971 was to sell a factory, an action partly forced by the discovery that the upper age of children buying or being bought toy cars had dropped from fifteen in the late 1950s to eleven, representing a dramatic reduction in the size of the market. The 1/36-scale Formula 1 racing cars of 1972, despite their excellent decals, have less collector appeal than earlier product. Nevertheless, Corgi's fortunes picked up, and the factory had to be expanded. Their 1/18-scale Formula 1 JPS was accompanied by a marketing tool, an educational 'Tramline Project Book showing how we can learn [road safety] from the Grand Prix Greats', illustrated with Corgi cars. Though its profits went up – partly as a result of the decline in sharpness of casting detail and decoration – sales volume dropped worryingly again. While there was some recovery, 1980 saw a dramatic fall in production and the first Corgi losses since 1971. Thereafter, the decline was virtually continuous. Shareholder rights issues, rationalization, the attempt to go into computers…nothing stemmed the flow of cash out of the company, and it was effectively closed in 1983.

Lesney was badly shaken by Mattel's introduction of its low-friction axles. These toys were direct competitors in the American market, which Matchbox had previously had to share only with Topper's Johnny Lightning. In the attempt to compete with the rolling success of Hot Wheels, there was a rapid change in the style of the 1–75 range. Soon, all had suspension and oversize wheels. Some collectors, deciding that the charm of the range had gone, quickly gave up collecting the toys or gradually ran out of enthusiasm. By deliberately producing colour and decal variations – technical variation collecting having been the life-blood of the Matchbox enthusiast – Lesney sought to encourage collectors and widen the market. On average, there were three totally new models per catalogue issue in the period 1965 to 1980, with about four changes in colour across the group. Multiplying these seven 'variations' by the seventy-five numbers in the range gives a total in excess of 500 'new' toys/models to be bought by the child or adult – a winning system. Yesteryears, which were increasingly being

bought by adults for themselves, were given the same treatment with, up until 1980 at least, pretty much the same success.

The scene in Britain at the time was dominated by the three manufacturers – Dinky, Corgi and Matchbox – but other firms were poking a toe in. Britains made – unusually for the period – a group of motorbikes in 1/32 scale; Lonestar modelled some 1/45-scale American prototypes (Corvair, Rambler and Sunliner), along with a Rolls, and DCMT/Impy tried to compete with Corgi Junior and the Matchbox 1–75s.

below: *The Tonka Quarry Dump Truck is an example of this smaller type of toy still being made in the 1970s (pressed-steel, 12cm/5in, c1970, USA).*

the beginning of the end of the road

FRENCH DECLINE AND RISE

French children had plenty of choice of toy cars. Even though Dinky in France was part of the Meccano empire and therefore involved in its take-over by Lines Bros, it was left alone and continued to act independently of England. Indeed, from 1965 a group of new 'Super Détail' models were made, adding a new dimension to the excellent existing range. They had opening doors, bonnets and so on, and covered a variety of types – from a Ferrari 275GTB, through Peugeots and the Citroën 2CV to Alfa Romeos. The opening parts fitted neatly and the paint finishes were good. New military

above: *The battery-operated Matchbox 5 Chevy Hot Rod Racer (plastic, 25cm/10in, c1985, China).*

models were produced at this time, but nothing was as awe-inspiring as the early 1960s Brockway Bridgelayer, which unfolds roadway before it. Among Dinky's general commercials was a spectacular yellow and red Pinder Circus GMC truck and trailer, which was partnered by a Peugeot 404 and Caravan. These two items come high on many collectors' want lists and are consequently very expensive compared with the average run of toys produced at this time. The 1400 series of super-detailed cars and racing cars culminated in 1971 in a catalogue that featured the Citroën Présidentielle on its front cover. The exquisite grey finish of President de Gaulle's official

car, the special DS, makes this most desirable piece a fitting swansong for French Dinky, which no longer could deny the economic problems around it. Winding down in the first half of the 1970s, it revamped models to keep it going until it shipped some of the dies to Spain, where, until 1981, cars were made for French Dinky by Pilen. In 1980, it turned to Solido for a short time to make simple models, dubbed Cougar, for them.

Solido continued to produce the 100 series, with all its different types of car, truck, military vehicle, and the veteran and vintage types they had recently introduced. The gradual demise

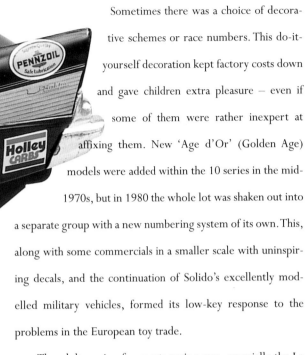

Sometimes there was a choice of decorative schemes or race numbers. This do-it-yourself decoration kept factory costs down and gave children extra pleasure – even if some of them were rather inexpert at affixing them. New 'Age d'Or' (Golden Age) models were added within the 10 series in the mid-1970s, but in 1980 the whole lot was shaken out into a separate group with a new numbering system of its own. This, along with some commercials in a smaller scale with uninspiring decals, and the continuation of Solido's excellently modelled military vehicles, formed its low-key response to the problems in the European toy trade.

The adult passion for sports racing cars, especially the Le Mans cars in France, prompted Safir to change direction in 1971. Gone were the old-time veteran models. In came the latest Lola, Porsche and Ferrari in a variety of different sponsor liveries. Marketed as Champion, they – like JEP's models in earlier times – had a plastic body on a diecast chassis. Such was the quality that you could not tell what they were made of until you felt that the upper part was warm while the lower was cold. (You can usually tell if a part is plastic or metal by the way it feels if you hold it against your cheek, no matter what the ambient temperature.) The quality and authenticity of the decals were excellent. In the late 1970s, Safir issued a range of all-metal Formula 1 racing cars and also a few in 1/20 scale, including the Citroën 11BL and Alpine. Its light commercial

of French Dinky, however, opened up the market for models of French saloons and estates, of which Solido took full advantage. Its catalogues from the first half of the 1970s contain the evidence. The 1972 100 series production was boosted in the 1973 catalogue by an Alpine 310 GT, a Citroën GS, a Ligier JS3 LM, a Renault 17TS and three non-French cars. The new series 10 began with a Renault 5, a Peugeot 104 and two Matras. To brighten up these good basic castings, Solido sold sheets of decals. Some of the spectacular Le Mans cars were supplied with all the decals fitted; others had them attached to the side that showed through the box window, with the ones for the other side and fitting instructions supplied in the packaging.

vehicles shared the good-quality decals.

Norev turned from plastic to metal in the early 1970s, producing prolific quantities of very fine, light castings. It kept some of the old dies in production but now made the toys in metal. Its plastic 'Moyen Age' models of cars from the 1920s and 1930s were sold off, to become the nucleus of the metal Eligor range in 1976. Norev continued to make toys, and then turned to producing many promotionals and 'specials'. These are models commissioned by a firm or individual for resale to celebrate an event, rather than as a promo for the firm whose name is on the side. This successful side of the business is still in operation. Eligor went on to produce a very wide range of cars and vans, with advertising aimed directly at the collector. Majorette was founded in 1966 by M. Veron, whose name (turned back to front) was the origin of the name Norev, to produce toy vehicles for youngsters. These 1/60-scale diecasts towed trailers and had other features to enhance their play value. Road sections, filling stations and figures were all added later. Additional scales, larger at 1/24 and smaller at HO, were brought in to expand the range. There was, and still is, a great emphasis on point-of-sale display units, and the toys can be found in small shops, large supermarkets and airports. These are toys aimed squarely at children and are not often collected.

Mention must also be made of France Jouets (FJ), which made 1/45-scale diecast military and commercial vehicles between 1959 and 1969. To begin with, it made neatly cast GMC trucks in many guises, then followed with Willys Jeeps

and a good series of Berliet Stradair trucks. A selection of the dies was subsequently used by Safir in the 1970s, with both metal and plastic.

GERMANY WAVERS

Even in Germany, the strongest European economy during the 1970s, experienced a similar shrinking of the toy industry. Even though there were no financial crises – indeed, the Deutschmark was going from strength to strength – the population trends were the same: the baby boom was over, so there were fewer children in the target age group; and the upper limit of that group was lowering, as diecast toys were put aside for more interesting teenage pursuits. The market was shrinking, and that was that. Märklin continued its range, gradually deleting old models (cars first and then the commercials), so that the early group was gone by the mid-1970s. At the same time, it was replacing them with the 1800 series, with the current standard features, including interiors, opening doors and suspension. There was a marketing tie-in with Mercury from Italy, and for a time both ranges were found in the same catalogue. Similarly, in another agreement, Märklin and Tekno were featured in the same Danish catalogue. By 1977, however, cars (including Märklin's own slot-car system) had ceased to be made.

Schuco made a series of thirteen German cars in 1/43 scale from the early 1970s. By varying the liveries – ADAC, Taxi, Police, Fire Chief, and so on – it stretched the

DINKY TOYS *super rapide* SPEEDWHEELS **CITROËN PRESIDENTIELLE**

above: *The beautifully designed Citroën DS Presidential Limousine was the last toy made at the French Dinky factory (15cm/6in, 1970, France).*

catalogue numbers to thirty. These rather stolid castings are not much sought-after outside Germany. There was a 'financial break' in 1977, but they were made for only two years or so after its return. These did not sell, and stocks lay around on shop shelves for years. During the same period there was a 1/66-scale series of diecast cars with opening doors, based on German and other prototypes that are particularly sought-after by collectors of small-scale vehicles. At the other end of the scale, Schuco continued with the types of battery-powered and radio-controlled cars that had always been its forte. Though good toys, these have not sparked a major following. The whole of the Schuco group soon went into liquidation.

RW-Ziss was brave enough to start up in 1963, making most of its product in the second half

of the decade. Its old-timers fell into two distinct groups; RW were nicely detailed, while Ziss were a bit rough-and-ready, approximately the quality of Rami in France. Since the early 1970s, NZG has been making diecast trucks and earth-moving equipment (scrapers, diggers, and so on) in a variety of scales. However, it is a difficult group to classify. Although they are suitable as toys, they are very expensive excellent models that look as if they were promotionals, and not initially aimed at the collectors' market. If you want to collect plant, however, you can hardly do better. Gama continued to make some reasonable vehicles, but concentrated on the toy market with motorized, remote-steering, large-scale versions. Siku made some diecast

1/27 vehicles but also continued as before with 1/32, 1/55 and 1/60 toys. Many have working features and are quite delicate castings. However, perhaps because of the strength of the mark, they were expensive to buy as toys; and, despite their undeniable quality, have failed to find a following outside Germany – a fact not helped by an inefficient distribution system. Cursor's products, in nicely detailed 1/43-scale plastic, were never intended as toys. They were models of early Mercedes and Benz, intended to be sold in the Stuttgart museum shop, and are thus a hybrid between promotionals and models for the collector. Of all the companies that produced small-scale series, ever-popular in Germany Wiking was taken over by Siku in 1984. As Wiking faded from the scene, Herpa became the best known make. Made in 1/87 scale, these mainly German prototype cars, buses and other-commercials were aimed specifically at (railway) modellers and collectors.

OLD NAMES AND NEW

By 1970, the quality of the new models of the Danish Tekno was falling a little, perhaps as a consequence of its founder's death the previous year. The next couple of years were most complicated. Some of the late production, made while the company was owned by Lange Legetøj, has the Tekno logo blanked out. After the factory closed, some models (Volvo saloons, for example) were assembled elsewhere from parts. The quality of these is not so good; there are often no boxes, and the provenance is unclear. Transfers for some of the trucks were also 'rescued' and used to refurbish old models or finish new ones. Care should be taken in buying anything from this era. In 1972, Tekno's assets were sold to a Dutch company that concentrated on the Eurotrailer trucks, but also made some smaller ones, as well as a Saab 99. These are all marked 'Made in Holland', carry authentic liveries and are

below: The Asahi 1950 Buick Coupé was issued with its own license plate number and ownership registration (tinplate, 27cm/11in, c1980, Japan).

popular with truck drivers and commercial vehicle collectors. Similarly, and appealing to the same market, Lion Car concentrated on large box trailers and trucks with very high-quality advertising decals. At this time, Belgium was known only for Sablon, a 1968 range of nine 1/43-scale diecast cars that was available in shops, but was also adopted as promotionals by the Jacques chocolate manufacturers.

In Italy, Mercury continued to make 1/43-scale diecasts but there was a flood of new names. Politoys, which had been making plastic toys, began – in a pleasant change – a new metal series in 1965 that was accurate and of good quality. Its Penny series dates from 1966. Later its name changed to Polistil. Mebetoys, which became a part of Mattel, started making toys of the same high quality in 1967, though this had fallen off somewhat by the end

below: A Saratov RAF Minibus with special decoration for the 1980 Moscow Olympics (diecast mazac, 11cm/4.5in, c1980, USSR).

of the 1970s. Edil made a few Italian cars. Pocher created a series of semi-promotional Fiat saloons – 500, 600, 1300 and 124, some in the odd scale of 1/13 – in the mid-1960s. Yaxon picked up on the enthusiasm for racing cars and, from 1978, made 1/43-scale diecast F1 cars. Brumm began its long reign in 1975. The founder of the company had been a part of Rio, and the story goes that there was a falling out and a lawsuit, which prevented him from starting up in competition for a specific length of time. At the first opportunity, he did so, beginning with a small series of historic steam road vehicles, using a lot of plastic. These were aimed at the collector, as were the 1/43-scale cars and the racing-car series, which is still being continued today.

New arrivals were the feature in Spain. Eko made a wide variety of very small 1/88-scale plastic cars, commercials and military vehicles. Though the mouldings are good, they are

not yet really collectable, as are its 1/43 veteran and vintage vehicles. Joal and Pilen both started making 1/43-scale diecast in 1968. The latter made ten Formula 1 cars that were good enlarged 'copies' of the Politoys Penny Toys. Road cars were added to the range in the 1970s, and there were some interesting choices of subject, nicely modelled, but some of the sports coupés were treated to a rather horrible plated finish. Most of Pilen's production was copied from elsewhere, though its manufacture from obsolete French Dinky dies was legitimate. It also was the source of late French Dinkies marked 'fab en Espagne'. Joal made good models, even if the early ones did appear to be copies of the Tekno E-Type Jaguar, among others. Later toys, however, including a wide range of commercials, were original. Metosul, from Portugal, had its origin in the Osul plastic toys of 1950–55, but it came to notice in 1966 with metal copies of Corgi, Dinky, Tekno and other manufacturers. Its main claim to fame is a Mercedes Benz 200 in various taxi versions, and an extensive selection of liveries on Atlantean double-decker buses. A brief fad among collectors,

these are now of interest only to some of the specialist bus enthusiasts. Production ceased in 1989.

As wealth spread around the world, so did toy cars. Gamda began production in Israel in 1965, making military and civilian subjects: some from the execrably bad English River Series; others, including a superb Willys Jeep, original. However, the mainly 1/43-scale range, is, on the whole, not good. Gamda, now branded as Sabra on the models, exported its own American cars, labelled as Cragstan, to America between 1969 and 1972. Buby of Argentina was using Solido dies under licence and also producing its own range of American cars. Nicky bought old Dinky Toy dies to make a series of poor, badly finished castings for the Indian market. There was a brief flurry of excitement among collectors when the first Novoexport/Saratov products appeared from the USSR in 1970. These are diecast models of Moskvitch, Gaz and other Eastern European makes. The saloons, brakes and so on are pleasant castings, though they tend to suffer from metal fatigue. Ironically, when the Iron Curtain came down and they became more readily available, the Western collector seemed to lose interest in them.

above: *A Chevrolet Corvette Stingray (11cm/4.3in, c1970, Israel) and a Chevrolet Police Car (11cm/4.3in, c1970, Israel).*

CHEGER

KATTUS

e Kost aus aller Welt.

| JM ⊗ | Johnson Matthey |
| KATALYSATOREN |

It is not easy to fit the automotive toys released over the past two decades into the context of the hundred years or so such toys that have been made, or to present a coherent story of this recent period. There is still manufacturing activity in countries throughout the world. Some toy companies have turned to producing only adult collectables; some have stayed resolutely manufacturers of children's playthings; others try to profit from the best of both worlds. And you never know what is around the corner, as more countries embrace capitalism, and their children become a market sector. One factor that is liable to distort perceptions about this period is the remarkable difference in the willingness of companies to hand out information. While some produce brochures in quantity, others are too busy making product to waste time answering questions. Still others are so busy protecting their trademarks – a most valuable commodity in the 1990s – that they seem obstructionist. Dealing with recent events also raises another problem: the latest episode can seem hugely important, whereas in fact the manufacturers and products of the late 1990s may be dwarfed in significance by something more exciting in the future.

ERTL

In America, Ertl has shown remarkable consistency in the quality of its product ever since, seemingly unaffected by the general problems in the toy market, it expanded its Dyersville plant in 1980. Along with an ever-developing farm-toy range, Ertl has made road and racing vehicles in scales ranging from 1/64 to 1/43 and 1/25. With keen awareness of what would be popular, it made both classic cars and popular race cars – many, such as that of Richard Petty, with accurate decalling. Its character merchandising vehicles – spin-offs from successful television series such as *The Dukes of Hazzard* and *The A-Team* – are marketing lessons in themselves. In January 1984, a double-sided full-colour *A-Team* flyer featured a 1/16-scale pressed-steel van and a Corvette; a 1/25 pressed-steel Peterbilt truck and trailer; a 1/48 pull-back van; a 1/64 diecast van and Jeep; a plastic radio-controlled van in 1/40; a plastic Corvette and van in large scale; and six other items, ranging from a plastic kit to a Wrist Racer – a little van attached to a wrist strap with a launching attachment.

The classic cars Ertl introduced in the first two years of the 1980s, most of which lasted in the catalogue for only two or three years, consisted of a mixture of European and American marques, ranging in date from 1948 (Jaguar XK120) to 1970 (Mustang Boss), but soon its product was entirely American. The 1984 catalogue included Nascars – made of plastic and metal and had a simple radio-controlled mechanism – ride-on tractors, construction toys in scales from 1/64 to 1/16, and funny toys for tots. Full-function radio-controlled cars were added later. This pattern of mixed materials over a wide range of products, with emphasis on character merchandising and race cars, led in the mid-1980s to no fewer than eighteen licensing arrangements being acknowledged.

By 1988, there were six flyers listing farm toys, and prod-

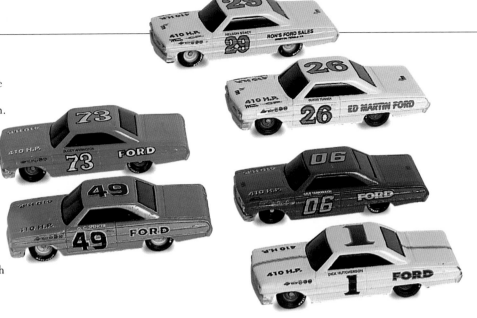

ucts were being aimed at specific markets; some were made available only in America, others only in Britain, and so on. The pre-school market was catered to, but still keen on accuracy, Ertl was making excellent models. Its Blueprint Replicas 1/43-scale '88 Fiero GT packaging tells us that the model was made in Korea and was 'Manufactured under licence of Pontiac Motor Division, General Motors Corporation'. The full sales pitch follows in a closely worded blurb:

Taking a spin in a hot '88 Fiero GT tells you this car is styled for performance. The famous Tech IV engine has a new secondary force balance system to smooth and quiet engine operations, and the new suspension is designed from the frame up to enhance ride and handling...

Impressive! Is Ertl trying to sell you a toy, a model or the full-size car? Among its 1990s 1/12- and 1/18-scale diecast Muscle Cars, the increasingly wacky full-size liveries were reflected in, for instance, the 1970 Hemi 'Cuda decorated in Plum Crazy Purple and the AAR 'Cuda in Vitamin C Orange with black stripes. The 1997 Ford F150 is finished in a classier Moonlight Blue. The 1/18-scale STP Pontiac Grand Prix is a beautiful model finished in the silver paint scheme specially designed for the 1996 season of the Daytona 500 to celebrate the twenty-five-year association between Richard Petty and STP. Ertl's policy, developed over fifty years, is to appeal to every age group and to every enthusiast for things on four wheels.

above: Racing Champions Ford Fastback Racing Car in different liveries (mazac, 8cm/3in, c1992, China).

RACING CARS

The zeal for racing cars is worldwide, with circuits in America, Europe, Australia and Japan, but the US has such a passion for the sport that many different series have developed. While the Daytona 500 is the race of legend, heralding the start of the season, it is not in fact the earliest of the races, which go on somewhere in the vast country from February to November. Races have been developed for any and all types of vehicle, from road

above: A Chevrolet Camaro Z28 by Zeetoys with a pull-back motor (diecast, 10cm/4in, c1982, Hong Kong).

cars through heavy articulated trucks to specially developed, types that create new race categories. The successful drivers have become famous, and sponsors (from STP to McDonald's) use the vehicles as mobile advertising billboards, often changing the decoration from race to race. The toys produced in response, as always, have mirrored the real world – trucks, hot rods, sprint cars, pro-stockers, dragsters, and funny cars have all been modelled in a variety of scales from 1/64 to 1/24. As the sport became more and more commercialized, with famous drivers and advertisers tying up their names as trademarks and making licensing agreements, so the system was extended to toys. No longer was a firm happy to allow its logo to be used to secure free advertising. It wanted to be paid for the use of its name, claiming that a toy with fictitious decalling would not sell as well as one with a popular real name, and that the owner of the name deserved a slice of the cake. The twenty-

five to thirty years of this development have been mirrored by the changes in hobby types from one predominantly collecting toys to, increasingly, collecting models.

Ertl was not the only existing toy manufacturer to make race cars. Matchbox and Mattel did, too. Hot Wheels was a range ideally suited to take advantage of the developments in racing over the past thirty years, and Mattel, moving into sponsorship itself, could now make a Hot Wheels toy of a car carrying the Hot Wheels logo! Currently, under the Pro Racing label, it is catering to the toy trade, with $2 bubble-packed toys, and to the collector, with a deluxe version of the same vehicle with rubber tyres and better tampo, at up to three times as much. Mattel's latest innovation is about as up-to-the-minute as possible. Its Computer Cars are bubble-packed on to the backing card, along with an interactive disc, compatible with Microsoft Window that contains three short 'game/ drives'. Some of the early Hot Wheels are worth considerable sums, but even a current issue can suddenly become highly desirable and shoot up in price. The Pro Racing label was to be launched at the Daytona 500, but full stocks were not ready, so the first products were rushed. Some were packed the wrong way around in the bubble packaging, an accidental variation that makes them scarce and therefore worth more. One product, over which there was a hitch in the licensing agreement, was subsequently withdrawn, and this even greater scarcity has resulted in a still higher price.

below: A Richard Petty STP Car (c1991, China), a Matchbox Ford Thunderbird (c1991, Thailand) and a Matchbox Buick Le Sabre (c1987, Macau).

FAR EASTERN MANUFACTURERS

The distant diecasting factories of Hong Kong had increasingly been contracted by American and European manufacturers to make products for inclusion in their own ranges, labour costs being so much lower there that the increased transport costs could be absorbed. In the mid-1970s, however, the names of Hong Kong manufacturers began to appear on toy vehicles that were sold in supermarkets in Europe, in outlets such as Woolworth in Britain and primarily in chains such as K-Mart in the US. Some of these were commissioned, and others were sourced by importers. Typically, they were cheap when they were available, had speed wheels of varying types and were of variable quality. Playart made toys with rather ill-fitting doors in about 1/40 scale, picking cars from all over the world. Tintoys, whose catalogue numbers are prefaced WT, made classic, sports and modern cars. Universal, Lucky Toys and Wildwheels made for Cragstan are names you may come across, though they are often found only on the packaging, which enables the series name to be changed with ease for a different market.

Ideal made a good line in steeds for Evel Knievel, the stunt motorcyclist, as well as dragsters and Nascar-style stock cars. Wondrie Metal made some reasonable-enough-for-the-price 10cm (4in) -long pull-back classic cars in the mid-1980s, some nasty ones half the size, and a range of American cars that came 'freewheel', 'pull back' or 'leaping'! Summer Metal Products made a wide range of vehicles, including truck rigs and fire

above: *The Road Champs Elgin Pelican Street Cleaner (diecast/plastic, 9cm/3.5in, 1993, China).*

engines. Yatming toys were made in Hong Kong and distributed by Norev in 1988, but by 1989 they were being manufactured in Thailand, where they made copies of Tomica. The Welly range was first made in Hong Kong and later in China, and at the end of the decade it was being given away with petrol in Britain. These are just a few examples from what could be lengthy catalogue of names.

Some ranges have been made entirely in the Far East but have their registered addresses in the US. Zylmex and Zee marked their metal toys and seem to have made their product for K-Mart in 1980 at least. Zylmex's small-size Dynamights include these unlikely companions: Citroën, Honda 600, Cement Mixer and Fire Engine. Zee made a selection of Grippers: Wheelies, with good castings, some with tampo-printed decals with pull-back motors that will do a wheelie at the end of their run; Classics, Explorers and Formula 1 cars. Zee are still increasing their ranges. Road Champs – which

above: *The Yatming 1923 Ford Coupé with a pull-back action motor (diecast, 11cm/4.5in, c1990, Hong Kong).*

include some excellent diecast and plastic mouldings of trucks, with attractive tampo decals, and a complex road sweeper – are marketed around the world. Hartoy, making 1/64-scale classic 1940s and 1950s trucks in period liveries announced a price reduction at the 1997 British Toy Fair.

THE COLLECTORS' MARKET

The year 1981 marked the beginning of the virtual demise of toy vehicle production outside of the Far East, with the exception of France, Italy, and one or two other small pockets, as the world market swung towards producing models for collectors. These satisfy the collectors' demand for greater accuracy and more detail, and the price is inevitably higher. Resin and white metal allow high-quality, small-series, specialist production at a reasonable cost,

right: *Diapet made this rare and unusual Honda Stream Motor Scooter (10cm/4in, 1984, Japan).*

but by the time the vehicles have been hand-finished, as small production runs dictate, the cost of manufacture can shoot up. Large manufacturers, instead of trying

to make a profit out of manufacturing what the child or man in the streets wants, are increasingly making something first and then trying to convince the public that they want it, through the use of limited editions and special marketing schemes.

Although some firms do not make limited editions that are advertised as such, a deliberate shortness of supply keeps collectors' interests fired up. Promotionals are issued by petrol stations, and marketing devices make sure that stocks of less desirable pieces are sold: the inclusion of one exclusive item in a set, for instance, means that the collector is obliged to buy the whole package to obtain the one that is really wanted. Racing Champions have been in the 1/64 market for some time, and it, Pit Road and others have paid for a licence from race organizations such as Nascar and print the year's events list on the back of their packaging. Revell, perhaps better known as a plastic-kit manufacturer, is now in this growth area as well. A name from the past, Johnny Lightning, is being used to market a line of limited-edition models that can claim to be genuinely limited, because the company announces

the length of the run on the box and numbers each vehicle. Despite their name, these are not toys but are directly aimed at the collector. K-Mart has joined the system and, next to the toys on its shelves, you can find limited editions that are not numbered but are limited only to the number it has decided to commission. Woolworth has its own line of racing Haulers, made, as is most of this type of product, in China.

Collectors frequently gather at the swapmeets, expositions, bourses, or toy shows – the names vary around the world. There are clubs you can join to make sure you get the latest issue of almost anything 'collectable', at a price set at what it is considered the market will stand. Price guides are essential for the beginner, as are those magazines that are independent of the organizations with a vested interest in promoting collectables. Knowledge is important. For instance, if you collect Hot Wheels, it is essential that that you know all about the twenty wheel types. One magazine that is independent (except of course that it needs to attract paid advertising to survive) carries the following ad:

above: *Matchbox Chevrolet Corvettes (diecast, 8cm/3in, c1981-86. UK and Macau).*

Be your own boss...earn big money selling all lines of NASCAR collectibles. I can show you how *you* can become a Dealer and where you can sell your products to hundreds of hungry collectors...how you can tap into this new market that is just exploding with each passing day. Don't miss the train. Get aboard today & start earning that extra money you need easily...

CAUTION!
Due to small parts, not recommended
for children under three years old.

FROM TOYS TO MODELS

In Britain, when Corgi was rescued from the financial collapse of Mettoy by a management buy-out, it immediately started the shift from toys to models, though it kept some of the toys in 1/35 and 1/43 scale, as well as the Junior range, in production. In 1985, it reissued four Corgi Classics – Rolls-Royce, Bentley, Ford Model T and Renault – each in three different colours. Thereafter, there was a rapid expansion into the collectors' market and an accompanying reduction in its toy output. The take-over by Mattel in 1990 provided much-needed financing for the plethora of new collectors' models in a wide range of liveries. Specialization continued, with a growing emphasis on buses. All the new ideas, many concentrating on limited editions, were aimed directly at the collectors' market. The tie with Mattel was brief, for in 1995 another management buy-out divorced the two, enabling Corgi to make exclusive arrangements with UK bus companies for using their liveries and to concentrate entirely on models for the collector.

Matchbox's difficulties were solved when it was purchased by the Universal Toy Company of Hong Kong in 1982. The Yesteryear range was marketed as Matchbox Collectibles, but the small Matchbox 1–75 toys were still aimed at children. The Dinky name was bought in 1988 for its nostalgia value, and in the hope that the desirability that the old toys had developed would rub off on the new, Macau-manufactured Dinky Collection, a range of classic

left: *A Fuel Tanker by Hess with the tanker acting as a money box and battery-operated electric lights (plastic, 33cm/13in, 1984, Hong Kong).*

sport and saloons aimed at the collector. A new name on the scene, Lledo, was created by reversing the last name of Jack Odell, formerly of (and one of the originators of) Matchbox, in 1983. Its six toys-cum-models harked back to the beginning of Matchbox and Yesteryear, with five of them being horsedrawn vehicles. Very soon, special liveries and promotionals were featured on a small series of basic castings, not to any particular scale. Any pretence that they were toys was soon dropped. The packaging was still marked 'not suitable for a child under 3 years' – suggesting that they were toys for older children – but the statement is actually a safety regulation. Vanguards, a range of 1950s and 1960s English cars and light commercials, was introduced in the 1990s to compete in the nostalgia market. This area of appeal was widened in 1997 with a merchandising tie-in with Coca-Cola .

Solido is the French example. Its vintage and classic cars were originally conceived as just another type of toy car in the gamut of its production of racing cars, saloon cars, old cars, but increasingly during the 1970s it realized the potential of the adult buyer. In 1980, Solido marketed its Age d'Or (Golden Age) range separately, aiming it directly at the company's existing following of adult collectors. Solido is still going strong, owned since 1981 by the toy manufacturers, Minialuxe. It was one of the first to realize the commercial importance of the collector. Many of the Minialuxe dies were reused in the 1980s and 1990s by Solido itself, and others were released under the Verem label. When the first group of Golden Age was

re-released, Solido dropped the price and retailers and collectors found that they had paid more for models in the past than they could buy them for in the present. This led to the continuing debate about the effect that reissues have on toy values. Solido made a small group of saloon cars for Dinky at one point very late in that firm's life. All these models are correctly marked underneath, but their similarity and the multitude of reissues can cause confusion among the unwary. Norev, who was still making promotional vans, later joined up with Solido/Minialuxe for a joint marketing operation.

Germany was left, after Siku's take-over of Wiking in 1984, with two toy manufacturers. Siku itself became the more prolific, continuing to make good-quality diecasts, in several scales that were well finished in bright colours and with a variety of action features. Gama, still a little uninspired, concentrated on 1/24-scale tractors, old-timers and a range of 1/43-scale cars, including a group of semi-promotional Opels. Schabak, which had come to the fore after buying some of the Schuco dies when that company failed, made good contemporary 1/43 to 1/25 cars and light vans. In the expensive price range for a toy, they are often produced as promotionals for the motor trade. NZG are also in the promo market, making models of Porsche and superb contractors' plant. Conrad does the same making models for Audi and also high-quality, beautifully finished commercials and plant that are popular with collectors. Old Schuco dies are being used to produce new models. As a general rule, if they are fitted with rubber tyres, they are

originals; if the tyres are plastic, they are reissues and consequently of lesser value.

Many of the Italian toy companies are still in business,
producing toys of sufficient quality to be bought by collectors
as well. Polistil make 1/16-scale classics like MGA, Morgan,
etc., and modern and racing cars in almost every other size you
can think of down to 1/66 scale. Mercury and Mebetoys are
still manufacturing, both in 1/43, and the latter in the larger
1/25 scale as well. Burago, which had been making its same-
size classics – such as the Citroën 11BL, Jaguar XK120 and
modern racers like BMW and Ferrari, a type that is still continuing – created a most successful line of 1/18-scale classics in
1980. Finished in eye-catching colours and packed in classy
black window boxes, these are the epitome of, in marketing
jargon, 'perceived value' or, in plain speak, 'what a lot you seem
to get for your money'. Indeed, it is a bit of a puzzle how a
European company can make these to sell at such a compara-
tively low price. Standardization and volume of production
must form a major part of the answer. At the bottom end of the
Burago line, it makes cheap 1/43-scale cars, Saab and so on.

Firms such as Box have joined the other manufacturers aiming purely at the collector.

The Spanish companies Pilen and Joal,
are still in the toy business, the former making cars and the latter concentrating on a very
good, solid line in construction and farm machinery. In the
mid-1990s Joal made no cars or ordinary commercials, but
recently a few excellent castings have begun to appear, including one of a low loader carrying a helicopter. Vitesse, from
Portugal, is a major producer of highly detailed 1/43-scale
vehicles aimed at the collector. Some are sold under the Vitesse
name, but the firm also manufactures for many other brands.
Japan's major toy names, Diapet and Tomy, continue as before,
making competent castings. They have been joined by Shinsei,
which concentrates on 1/25 to 1/78-scale commercials and
construction equipment, modelling national brands. Japan
being a major manufacturer of full-size plant. Fifties, from the
decade the name suggests, produces Buicks, Thunderbirds, and
so on in 1/25 scale.

above: *Burago produce the Porsche 911 Carrera and Chevrolet Corvett – both are beautifully decorated models (diecast, 10cm/4in, 1997, Italy).*

TOY STORES

Recent visits to two stores with world-famous names were quite revealing. Toys'R'Us is almost entirely a true toy shop, selling many of the American brands mentioned in this chapter. Some of its items of stock are good examples of how automotive toys change, yet stay the same. Nylint and Buddy L are still making typical hook-and-ladder toys; Kenworth makes car transporters and the like, with electronic light and sound effects that almost outdo the full-size versions. There's even a Talk 'n' Go fire truck with a seventy-five-word vocabulary in fifty different random phrases, which operates at the press of a button. Kenworth's pedal cars range from baby push-and-ride plastic toys to battery-powered Jeeps and buggies suitable for ages five to nine. The top of the range costs more than you might pay for a ten-year-old full-size car, though the price pales into insignificance compared with that of the electric Mercedes 230SLK Sports, tractors and other

above: The ERTL Pontiac Fiero 88 Coupé in the Blueprint Replicas range (diecast/plastic, 10cm/4in, 1988, Korea).

vehicles on sale in the Mercedes-Benz main showroom in London.

Hamley's, the leading London toy store, has a mixture of toys and models for the collector. Though price is some guide as to which are which, it can help to tell by looking not just at the product, but also at the purchaser. Who is watching the radio-controlled demonstration? Is it the father or his son who decides which Scalextric slot car to buy next? Is that man who is consulting his female companion discussing the suitability of a model for a nephew – or for display in their own living-room?

THE TOY TRADE IN THE MID-1990s

How did the toy trade see itself in the mid-1990s? The British magazine *Toy Trader,* in its July 1995 issue, reviewed the current situation in the toy-vehicle field. According to information supplied to them by Mattel:

The vehicles market is a wide and diverse category ranging from the ubiquitous three-inch remote controls to slot car sets. Vehicles currently have about 11 per cent share of the total toy market with value worth in excess of £180m. Although it's more stable than many sectors within the toy industry, its diversity makes it difficult to establish just who is in the driving seat. Miniature vehicles dominate the sector with a 41 per cent share, and competition within this category is fierce, with lots of players producing similar products. Tough competition has led to a diversification into feature-led miniature vehicles and the more profitable high price vehicle accessories such as play sets.

The magazine reviewed the British market manufacturer by manufacturer and produced an assortment of gems of disparate information. Minichamps (which produces models for the collector) was sponsoring Benetton's Formula 1 team. Amerang was shortly to release a 1/18-scale Elvis Presley 1995 Pink Cadillac in conjunction with Graceland and Elvis Presley Entertainment. Note that these are not toys, yet they are featured in *Toy Trader*. Benjamin Toys was distributor for Tootsietoy Hard Body cars, trucks and farm vehicles, as well as Jaditoy diecast tractors, earth-movers and playsets. Majorette and Solido had signed licences to produce diecast models of the Mini, Triumph Spitfire and Range Rover. Kyosho had launched examples of MGB, Austin Healey and Triumph TR3, while

Mattel had Morris vehicles, Minis, and Range Rover. Siku, Europe's biggest-selling range of diecasts, had introduced over thirty new models that year (several of which were variations on their standard product), including a very smart cement mixer. The UK distributor for Siku was also handling the collectables, from Wiking and Roskopf and the railway accessory line from Busch. Majorette's wide range of vehicles included heavy-duty transporters and bulldozers, and could be bought as build-your-own-site sets. Its Turboom vehicle fires caps as it crashes and falls apart, while the Traffic Jammers – four American classic cars – play music when you press the bonnet. Coca-Cola and Cadbury's advertising was also featured.

Matchbox made a wide range of Motorcity playsets, one of

which has the police defending the city, with electronic sirens and crash sounds adding to the realism. Mattel – as ever – had Hot Wheels, and Road Maniax was its futuristic vehicle playset. Rico, in its radio-controlled range, had Raging Bull, a pickup truck with wheelie-action spins and hopping turns. Burago's newest item featured in the *Toy Trader* magazine was yet another Mercedes-Benz. Micro Machines from Toy Option, launched in 1987, have sold over a billion toys, with thirty-five per cent of boys between the ages of four and nine owning at least one. The latest addition to the Toy Option offerings is an Auto Dealership set, which has a rotating rooftop car carousel, a paint booth with colour-wheel preview, sliding showroom doors and a rotating vehicle platform. There is a list of Tomy products, including a radio-controlled car transporter that can carry fourteen diecast vehicles. Tyco have made a pickup truck, Fire Power, that can fire foam missiles up to 6m (20ft)!

In America, Hasbro, which own Tonka, stated in its 1995 annual report that 'Brands and product are king in the consumer products industry' and featured the concept 'edutainment' – an ugly portmanteau word that surely has a strong future in marketing, combining as it does the venerable idea of learning with play.

TOY FAIRS AND AUCTIONS

To see toys, collectors and dealers *en masse*, you can attend one of the many toy fairs that now occur almost every weekend all over the world. Their venues and times are published in the hobby magazines that are available in news stands, from specialist model shops or by subscription. Not only are these fairs a source of both toys and models, but they are one of the best ways of finding out what is available and gaining the lore that enables collectors to make wise purchases. There will be stalls at these meets selling replacement parts from old toys. However, it is also interesting to see the wide range of parts available – one gets a revealing insight into what may have been replaced on a toy being offered for sale. Maybe collecting toys is a hobby (though some may think of it as an investment), but it never makes sense to spend money unwisely or be caught out by a persuasive dealer, if you can help it.

In recent years, there has been a rise in the quantity of toys that are selling through auction. To begin with, it was mainly expensive pieces of early tinplate and cast iron that were considered near enough to antiques to be auctioned. As the popularity of collecting has grown, however, so the range of toys at auction has increased, coming far more up to date; the number of auctions has also increased. Many auction houses have a great deal of experience and describe the toys accurately, although even the most careful can make a mistake. Others, however, do not have the same expertise. It is worth bearing in mind that auction rules vary from country to country and that, even within one country, the regulations governing public auctions are very much stricter than those for private ones. Be careful. Buy what you like at a price you can afford. Take any future appreciation in value as a bonus, not a right. Enjoy yourself.

INTRODUCTION

The following section aims to provide information that will benefit collectors and first timers alike. An extensive glossary, split into three sections, explains the many manufacturing methods involved in automative toymaking, collectors' terminology and a more general glossary. Thereafter, the reader is supplied with a fascinating list of some of the most expensive prices ever paid for automotive toys. Last, and not least, a thorough list of useful addresses is provided, including the addresses of the major auctioneers, the many museums that include some of the classic toys, and leading collectors and dealers.

GLOSSARY

MANUFACTURING METHODS:

Cast Iron: The gravity casting of molten cast iron into moulds of pre-shaped, glued sand that are made round an original master.

Diecasting: Method using molten metal forced into hard steel dies under great pressure.

Injection Moulding: Similar to diecasting but with plastic material used instead.

Master: The prototype or original piece, often made by hand, giving the definitive shape for the part to be cast or moulded.

Mazac (UK): Zamac (US): This is an alloy of zinc with a small addition of aluminium and traces of copper and magnesium. This alloy is the base for most diecast models and toys.

Pressed Steel: Where heavy gauge steel sheet is cut and pressed into the shapes between male and female platens under great external pressure.

Rubber: Similar to diecasting but using a rubber mixture as the moulding material.

Tinplate: Similar to pressed steel but using a very much thinner gauge of material, usually tinplated, before use.

Wooden Toys: Usually made from carved wood, and then painted.

COLLECTORS' NOMENCLATURE:

Boxed: In the same box in which it left the factory.

Character Merchandising: Models, usually made under licence from a film or TV company, showing popular characters. They are used to increase the public awareness of the characters concerned. They are also known as spin-offs in commerce.

Chipped: Having its original paint but with some play wear. Often described as slightly or heavily chipped.

Decal: Decoration applied to a toy by the use of a water- or spirit-based slide transfer on a backing film.

Japanned: A decoration applied to a finished toy by using a very hard varnish, often black. This applies only to early toys and was not used significantly after about 1920. It originated in Japan, hence its name.

Lithographed: Decoration applied, usually to tinplate sheets, by a multi-colour, multi-stage printing process, where the decoration is applied to the flat surface before it is cut and shaped.

Metal fatigue: The expansion and apparent rotting of mazac toys when they expand and break. This is caused by the electrochemical action due to traces of lead and cadmium in the alloy making the model expand.

Mint: A model that is in the same condition as when it left the factory.

Promotionals: Models made or decorated with the specific aim of promoting a particular brand name, often a food or other consumable.

Reproduction: A newly manufactured model as a replica of an earlier piece, sometimes from the original tooling.

Restoration: The refurbishing, to a greater or lesser extent, of a damaged or worn toy to its original appearance, sometimes with the intent to deceive a future owner.

Tampo: Decoration applied to a toy by means of a pre-coloured transfer roller or stamp.

Three-rail/Two-rail: Toy trains terminology; three-rail has the current flowing through both running rails with return through a centre rail, two-rail has outward flow through one running rail and return through the other.

GENERAL MOTORING TERMS:

Artics (UK): Semi (US): Articulated truck rig, tractor with mounted semi-trailer.

Bonnet (UK): Hood (US)

Boot (UK): Trunk (US)

Cabriolet (UK): A body style with a folding hood, usually padded, and with glass wind-up side windows – also known as a 'convertible'.

Cam: A projecting pip on a shaft or wheel.

Commercials: Commercial vehicles, such as trucks, buses, vans, tankers, etc.

Dickey seat: An occasional seat that folds up out of the boot, using the bootlid as its back, also known as a 'mother-in-law seat', or 'rumble seat' (US).

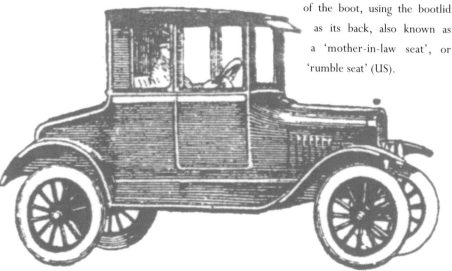

Dimestore: Shop where conventionally all items cost not more than a dime.

Doctor's coupé: An enclosed two-seat car body style, usually dating to before 1930.

Drophead coupé: *see* Cabriolet

Engine (UK): Motor (US)

Estate car (UK): Station wagon (US)

Flywheel: A heavy rimmed wheel designed to absorb rotational power.

Hood (UK): Top (US): The folding roof of a convertible or other openable car.

Kick panels: Panels for passengers to rest their feet on.

Landaulet: A closed car, the rear portion of which has a folding hood that could be opened in fine weather.

Leaf-spring suspension: Suspension by means of springs made up of several lengths of tempered steel laid together.

Limousine: A large, fully closed body style usually having a partition between the driver and the rear passengers.

Monocoque (UK): Unibody (US): A design where the body and chassis are combined into one structure giving better strength, and often cheaper to make.

Mudguards (UK): Splashguards (US)

Overriders: The vertical additions to front and rear bumpers to avoid cars over-riding each other in minor collisions and becoming locked together.

Peen: Use of a hammer to swell a rivet and, usually, produced a domed finish (as fixing the bases to toy cars).

Petrol (UK): Gasoline (US)

Play value: Modern jargon for how much a toy has been, or is perceived will be, played with.

Roadster (UK): An open two-seat sporting car, or 'runabout' (US).

Running board: Boards along the body sides to be used as steps to gain access to the interior, usually connecting the front and rear mudguards. They were also usually rubber-coated to avoid damaging the vehicle's paintwork. Not much used since about 1950.

Saloon (UK): A fully closed body style for four or more passengers – 'sedan' (US).

Semi-trailer: A trailer with axles at the rear only, the front is mounted onto the tractor unit.

Shooting brake (UK): Station wagon (US)

Silencer: (UK): Muffler (US)

Snorkel pumpers: Fire appliances with extending boom for the hose.

Spats: Half-round removable panels covering the rear wheels on some car designs. Used for aesthetic reasons.

Sulky: A two-wheeled horse drawn vehicle for one person.

Telescopic forks: Motorcycle front suspension with integral cylindrical springing and shock absorbers.

Tonneau: An early open-car body style; later, a waterproof cover for open cars seating areas.

Tourer: A four-seater open car.

Trade only: Sales to retailers only, not to the general public.

Vis-à-vis: Early open vehicles where the driver sits in the rear seat with the front passenger looking towards him, literally 'face-to-face' from the French originators of the design.

Windscreen (UK): Windshield (US)

Wing (UK): Fender (US)

TOYS — SOME TOP PRICES

DATE	LOT NUMBER	DESCRIPTION	PRICE REALISED	RECORD
May 1992		A rare tinplate Märklin four-volt electric ocean liner 'Augusta Victoria'	£42,000	Record for a Märklin boat
20 December 1994	Lot 21	Twenty-volt electric Swiss-outline 'Crocodile' articulated electric locomotive	£35,200	N/A
17 May 1990	Lot 489	A Märklin 00-gauge LMS E800 locomotive and tender	£24,200	N/A
20 December 1994	Lot 113	A steam triple-screw twin-funnel battle cruiser	£18,700	N/A
May 1991	N/A	A rare Märklin twenty-volt LMS R742 Passenger Train set, with original box	£15,400	Record for a single 00-gauge train set
October 1994	N/A	'Bentalls' delivery van Dinky Toy	£12,650	World record for a Dinky Toy
17 September 1997	Lot 327	A Märklin clockwork 4-4-0 MR locomotive No. 2609	£10,350	N/A
June 1994	N/A	'Blondin Cyclist'	£7,200	Record for a single Britains figure
17 September 1997	Lot 156	A rare prewar Dinky Toy 'H.G. Loose' promotional delivery van	N/A	N/A
19 September 1997	Lot 184	A Yonezawa 'Atom Jet' futuristic car	£4,370	N/A

A D D R E S S E S

MUSEUMS—UK

Abbey House Museum

Abbey Road

Kirkstall

Leeds

Yorkshire

LS5 3EH

England

Arundel Toy and Military Museum

23 High Street

Arundel

West Sussex

BN18 9AD

England

Bethnal Green Museum of Childhood

Cambridge Heath Road

London

E2

England

C. M. Booth Collection of Historical Vehicles

Falstaff Antiques

63–67 High Street

Rolvenden

Kent

TN17 4LP

England

Chester Toy and Doll Museum

12a Lower Bridge Street

Chester

Cheshire

CH4 8JW

England

Cotswold Motor Museum and Toy Collection

The Old Mill

Bourton-on-the-Water

Gloucestershire

GL54 2BY

England

The Cumberland Toy and Model Museum

Banks Court

Market Place

Cockermouth

Cumbria

CA13 9NG

England

Dewsbury Museum

Crow Nest Park

Heckmondwike Road

Dewsbury

West Yorkshire

WF13 2SA

England

Gloucester Folk Museum

99–103 Westgate Street

Gloucester

Gloucestershire

GL1 2PG

England

House on the Hill Toy Museum

Stansted Mountfitchet

Essex

CM24 8SP

England

Ironbridge Toy Museum

Banbury Road

Gaydon

Warwick

CV35 0BJ

England

The London Toy and Model Museum

21 Craven Hill

London

W2

England

Museum of Childhood

42 High Street (Royal Mile)

Edinburgh

Lothian

EH1 1TG

Scotland

Pickford's House Museum

41 Friargate

Derby

Derbyshire

DE1 1DA

England

Pollock's Toy Museum

1 Scala Street

London

W1

England

The Precinct Toy Collection

38 Harnet Street

Sandwich

Kent

CT13 9ES

England

Richmondshire Museum

Ryders Wynd

Richmond

North Yorkshire

DL10 4JA

England

The Sussex Toy and Model Museum

52–55 Trafalgar Street

Brighton

Sussex

BN1 4EB

England

Tintagel Toy Museum

Fore Street

Tintagel

Cornwall

PL34 0DD

England

The Toy Museum

Dedham Arts & Crafts Centre

The High Street

Dedham

Sussex

CO7 6AD

England

Antique Toy Museum

Exit 230, I-44

PO Box 175

Stanton

Missouri 63079

USA

Bauer Toy Museum

233 East Main

Fredericksburg

Texas

USA

Museum of Childhood

8 Broad Street

Greensport,

New York

USA

Museum of the City of New York

5th Avenue and 103rd Street

New York

NY

USA

Nashville Toy Museum

2613 McGavok Pike

Nashville

TN

USA

Remember When Toy Museum

Box 226A
Canton
Missouri
USA

Sullivan-Johnson Museum

223 North Main Street
Kenton
Ohio
USA

Toy and Soldiers Museum

1100 Cherry Street
Vicksburg
Mississippi
USA

Toy Train Museum

Paradise Lane
Strasburg
Pennsylvania
USA

Washington Doll's House & Toy Museum

5236 44th Street, NW
Washington, DC 20015
USA

CHRISTIE'S ADDRESSES

Christie's South Kensington

85 Old Brompton Road
London
SW7 3LD
England

Christie's

8, King Street
London
SW1Y 6QT
England

Christie's Scotland

164–66 Bath Street
Glasgow
G2 4TG
Scotland

Christie's Amsterdam

Cornelis Schuytstraat 57
1071 JG Amsterdam
The Netherlands

Christie's Geneva

8, Place de la Taconnerie
1204 Geneva
Switzerland

Christie's Rome

Palazzo Massimo Lancelotti
Piazza Navona 114
00186
Rome
Italy

Christie's New York

502 Park Avenue
New York
New York 10022
USA

Christie's East

219 East 67th Street
New York
New York 10021
USA

OTHER AUCTION-EERS' ADDRESSES

Bill Bertoia Auctions

2413 Madison Avenue
Vineland
NJ 08360
USA

Bill Bertoia Auctions

65–69 Lots Road
London
SW10 0RN
England

Hake's Americana & Collectibles

PO Box 144N
Pennsylvania 17405
USA

Mapes Auctioneers

1600 Vestal Parkway West
Vestal
NY 13850
USA

Phillip's

101, New Bond Street
London
W1Y 0AS
England

Phillip's Bayswater

10 Salem Road
London
W2 4DL
England

Phillip's New York

406 E. 79th Street
New York
NY 10021
USA

Richard Opfer Auctioneering, Inc.

1919 Greenspring Drive
Timonium
MD 21093
USA

Sotheby's London

34–35 New Bond Street
London
W1A 2AA
England

Sotheby's New York

1334 York Avenue
New York, NY 10021
USA

LEADING COLLECTORS AND DEALERS

Tony and Jack Grecco

Mechanical Banks, antique toys
2413 Madison Avenue
Vineland
NJ 08360
USA

Bill Bertoia

Toy soldiers and related items
PO Box 3490
Poughkeepsie
NY 12603
USA

Jim and Patsy Carlson

Schoenhut Collectors
7939 Cabarfae Trail
Clarkson, MI 48348
USA

Carl Lobel

Toys of all eras
Box 74A
Warren
VT 05674
USA

I N D E X